The Home Team

The Home Team

GOD'S GAME PLAN FOR THE FAMILY

CLINT ARCHER

Shepherd Press
Wapwallopen, Pennsylvania

The Home Team
© 2014 by Clint Archer

Trade Paperback ISBN: 978-1-63342-084-7

eBook ISBN
Mobi format: ISBN 978-1-63342-086-1
epub format: ISBN 978-1-63342-085-4

Published by Shepherd Press
P.O. Box 24
Wapwallopen, Pennsylvania 18660

This book is published in association with The Benchmark Group, Nashville, TN. *benchmarkgroup1@aol.com*

Page design and typesetting by Lakeside Design Plus
Cover design by Tobias' Outerwear for Books

First Printing, 2014
Printed in the United States of America

BP 22 21 20 19 18 17 16 15 14
14 13 12 11 10 9 8 7 6 5 4 3 2 1

Library of Congress Control Number: 2014942836

eBooks: www.shepherdpress.com/ebooks

Contents

Introduction: One Flesh, One Team   7

1   Team Rivals: Age-Old Opponents in New Uniforms   13

2   Team Basics: Know the Game   27

3   Team Captain: Dad, Play Your Position   41

4   Team MVP: Leader in Assists   55

5   Team Players, Part 1: Little League   71

6   Team Players, Part 2: Minor League   85

7   Team Solo: Singleness and the Family of God   101

8   Team Supporters: Para-Family Support   115

9   Team Huddle: The Family that Prays Together   129

Conclusion: Rating Greatness   143

Epilogue: Practice Makes Perfect   149

Notes   151

Introduction

One Flesh, One Team

Table tennis is a fun pastime for millions, but a dedicated few take the sport very seriously. When I play, I lean against the table and idly pat the ball back and forth while chitchatting with my fellow player. But professionals appear locked in mortal combat, brandishing their paddles like weapons of warfare and smashing the little ball with fervor. If you've ever watched such a spectacle, you've probably noticed that skilled players position themselves several steps away from the table: the more heated the bout becomes, the further apart the competitors move.

When I counsel married couples, I often refer to conflict between them as "table-tennis syndrome." To me, the sport provides an apt metaphor for the tension that exists in most marital counseling sessions: two rivals facing a taut net of animosity, distanced by an issue they don't really want to touch, deftly lobbing snide remarks at each other. The more they snap at each other, the further apart they drift.

My first office had an enormous three-seater sofa in it. When couples came in for marriage counseling, I began to notice a correlation between the severity of the tension between them and how they sat on the sofa. If the couple came in and sat together, possibly even holding hands, I knew that they viewed themselves as part of the same team, there to address a problem they both feared would get between them. But if the husband and wife sat on opposite sides of the sofa, leaving an obvious gap between them big enough to accommodate an invisible sumo wrestler, I guessed I was dealing with two opponents who viewed *each other* as the problem.

This simple table-tennis test proved remarkably accurate, and I learned that the first counsel I needed to give involved turning to

Genesis 2 and reminding couples of God's most foundational principle in his design for marriage and family—namely, the one-flesh union of a husband and wife.

The Cure for Table-Tennis Syndrome

In my experience, too few married couples have heard and understood that God considers them one flesh, joined permanently through a covenant. Thus, few couples know that God wants spouses to play as a team, facing problems together and never letting challenges get between them. This team mentality, starting with spousal one-flesh unity, is the cure for table-tennis syndrome. When a family closes ranks and functions as a close-knit unit for God's glory, it can withstand any challenge that comes. This may include issues with children, in-laws, finances, health, or any other trouble we face in a sin-cursed world. But if the husband and wife—the basic unit of the family—view each other as rivals, or label their kids as the problem, the family has little hope of making progress until they repair that misconception.

The biblical principles in this book are those that I've seen help my own family and families in my church. Simply put, we have found that **God's Word is sufficient and his grace abounds when we commit to following his design for the family**. The Bible explains clearly what a family is and what it should do. It also defines the roles of husband, wife, and children while describing the relationship between family and church, in-laws, schools, and other community factors. God's Word warns us about challenges that will come as a result of the curse and indwelling sin. The only way to pursue the blessings and protection that God intends for families is by understanding and implementing God's design for the family.

Team Talk

You don't have to be an athlete or even a fan to find the metaphor of a sports team helpful for understanding the family dynamic. Families, just like sports teams, must understand their goals and their opponents. Every member of the family must know his or her position and the rules of the game. And the family needs to understand the consequences of poor play as well as the rewards of fair play. Thinking about the "home team" this way can help us see what turns a group of related people into a real family.

Of course, the family matters far more than any game we could play. God's glory, the blessings that come from obedience, the negative consequences that result from disobedience—these significant spiritual realities are at stake in every family. So we must strive to know and obey God's will. If we rely on his grace and guidance, we can enjoy the wonderful blessing that God intended family to be. Conversely, if we try to change the rules or invent our own way of doing family, we may end up hurting ourselves and others, possibly with eternal consequences.

In this book I have assumed that the Bible is God's Word, and I have aimed my instruction at those who believe in Jesus as our only Lord and Savior. The title *Lord* implies that Jesus has the right to tell us how he wants us to live; he does this through the Bible. The title *Savior* implies that Jesus saves completely sinners who cannot help themselves with their own sin problem. If you do not acknowledge these realities, you will find that the principles in this book have no value for you.

Nobody's Perfect . . . Yet

On July 18, 1976, fourteen-year-old Nadia Comăneci represented Romania in the gymnastics team event. Spectators watched in riveted silence as she confidently completed a mesmerizingly ambitious and astonishingly flawless routine on the uneven bars . . . until the instant her feet planted an unfaltering dismount, which generated an avalanche of applause. But the jubilation dissipated suddenly when her result appeared on the digital display: Comaneci's brilliant performance had scored only 1.0.

In gymnastics, a panel of judges rates each performance according to its difficulty, creativity, and the technical proficiency of its execution. The highest and lowest figures are discarded and the final score represents an average of the remaining numbers. The highest number a judge can give is a perfect 10, and every judge would need to give a 10 in order for the cumulative score to be 10. Because this is so unlikely, the electronic score board only allowed space for a single digit on the left side of the decimal point: the maximum number it could show was 9.9, which means it displayed Comaneci's score as 1.0 instead of the perfect 10 the judges had awarded for the first time in Olympic history. An apologetic voice over the public address system explained the error and the crowd roared to ovation.

Little Nadia was—gymnastically speaking—the world's first perfect woman.

Of course, gymnastic perfection is determined subjectively by other people. In the spiritual realm, however, the standard of perfection is not subject to human opinion. God alone sets the standard of righteousness and judges whether it as been attained. In Matthew 5:48, Jesus said, "Be perfect, as your heavenly Father is perfect." Yet the reality is that "all have sinned and fall short of the glory of God" (Romans 3:23). As soon as mankind fell in the garden of Eden, God's standard became utterly unattainable.

Until Jesus.

When Jesus of Nazareth was born into this world, humanity encountered the first and only perfect person. That man lived a normal life on earth and in society. He submitted to government authorities, civil regulations, and the Mosaic law—systems that existed to manage moral imperfection. And Jesus was able to keep God's law perfectly. He never sinned and thus never fell short of God's perfect righteousness (Hebrews 4:15). Jesus offered his spotless life on the cross as a substitute for the sin of all who would trust in him for salvation: "For our sake he made him to be sin who knew no sin, so that in him we might become the righteousness of God" (2 Corinthians 5:21). This is the good news of perfection attained, as well as perfection imputed to every imperfect person who trusts in Jesus. So we can respond to this gift of salvation with worship and obedience. While we will not achieve perfection on earth as our Savior did, we can faithfully pursue the goal of glorifying God by God's grace. Every family has the great privilege of pursuing that goal together . . . as a team.

So before you read another paragraph or turn another page, please consider Jesus. Do not read this book for another list of ways to do marriage and family better: it's not intended as a rulebook or a checklist. If you read it like that, you will get frustrated and fail. You cannot accomplish any of the principles in this book apart from the Spirit of God applying grace to your failing heart. So seek Jesus and his grace. Then read on.

Abnormal Is the New Normal

There is no "normal" family, much less a "normal" godly family. Every family represents a unique collection of individuals, all with different relationships to the Lord. That said, I have written this book largely for families of professed believers since only believers will have the desire and ability, through the Holy Spirit, to implement what the Bible says we need to do. God's standard is the same for everyone—believer and unbeliever alike. Rather than provide endless permutations of all the variables (one spouse is unsaved, a child professes belief but shows no fruit, etc.), I opted to write for the ideal model. You readers must then apply these chapters to your unique situations.

How will you do that? First, believers will have the help of the indwelling Holy Spirit. Ask him for discernment. Second, believers should have the help of the church. If you are not already committed and serving members of a local church, I encourage you to become so and to avail yourself of the wisdom of your own pastors and spiritual leaders. A book like this is merely intended to help you think through issues and spur you on to love and good deeds, but it is no substitute for a local church body or the wisdom of a shepherd to whom God has entrusted you.

All that said, I trust that this book will be a blessing to you and your family, and that you will grow closer to one another and to the Lord for his glory and your good.

And . . . now that I have explained all the rules, let's sing the anthem and play ball!

1

Team Rivals

Age-Old Opponents in New Uniforms

The Himalayan kingdom of Bhutan is one of the most fascinating countries you could ever visit. Nestled on the border between China and India, Bhutan has gobsmacking scenery and a rich religious and political history including not a little internal and external turmoil. The national sport of archery has proud and ancient roots in defense and hunting, and their competitions display Bhutan's best in terms of athletic skill as well as food, song, and dance. A lifelong toxophilite (or fan of archery), I was fortunate to spectate one such competition in Bhutan's capital a few years back. Nothing I had yet seen in archery—or in sport, for that matter—could have prepared me for the experience.

Archery in Bhutan is different from anywhere else. For one thing, the target is not standard Olympic size (a 48-inch circle positioned 230 feet away). Instead, the rectangular target is 42 inches tall and 12 inches wide with an 11-inch bull's-eye standing an unbelievable distance of 430 feet away. That's like shooting an arrow at a dinner plate one and a half American football fields away from you.

And as if that wasn't hard enough, the archers aim through loud chaos. Olympic rules strictly forbid any deliberate distraction of archers: competitors may not even approach their own shooting line while an archer is at full draw. This respect of an opponent's concentration is a key courtesy in a sport that requires such intense focus. The Bhutanese, however, permit no shot to be made in silence. I guess they think it's no big deal to hit that target, so the fellow competitors loudly and incessantly heckle the archers. In fact, they stand perilously close to the miniscule target to raucously celebrate every miss and greet every hit with a sarcastic jig of feigned surprise. And by "perilously close," I mean that these vociferous scoffers stand *right in front of the target* while the archer takes aim, moving only moments before the arrow lands.

In real life, the competitive Bhutanese archers are usually great buddies. The heckling is considered a good-natured way of showing respect for opponents. The logic must run this way: "You know that I know that you are exceptionally skilled and focused, so you surely won't mind if I block the little target so far away from you and yell at you while you aim." To succeed, the archers must not only know their particularly difficult sport but also have the ability to maintain focus and ignore their opponents' efforts at subterfuge. Only if they can accomplish all of that do they have a chance at hitting their mark.

Families are like Bhutanese archers in a particularly rowdy competition. They must recognize the opposition they face and keep their eyes on their targets if they have any hope at success. We will begin this book, then, by naming exactly these challenges for families. We will first consider the intrinsic difficulty that the family faces in a sin-cursed world, and then we will examine a particular kind of interference that contemporary families face. Get ready to take aim.

Intrinsic Opposition to the Family

When a couple first gets married, they usually enjoy the doe-eyed optimism of a rosy future. They have big dreams of romance and cute kids and a fulfilling family life. Then, reality sets in. Marriage is unexpectedly difficult. Peace in the home can be fragile. Childrearing proves unpredictable and often unmanageable. It seems, at times, that absolutely nothing is going according to plan.

What is going on? It feels like something haunts the family, like the so-called "Curse of the Bambino" haunted the beleaguered Red Sox for eighty-six years after Babe Ruth was traded to the Yankees. It feels like all efforts to preserve any semblance of a happy family are useless in the face of life's intangible oppositions.

Some respond to these challenges by cynically questioning God, while others turn to the self-help section of the local bookshop. Still others sadly resign themselves to living in a dysfunctional situation or, worse, terminate the family bonds by divorce or abandonment. Maybe the family really isn't God's idea after all. It seems hopeless.

The problem is complex but not impossible to face. After all, the core problem is somewhat easy to name. The Bible teaches that the family itself is indeed God's design but that the individual roles within the family are under the curse of sin. Because of the fall of man, the world we live in has been cursed with difficulty and the roles we have been given are now cursed with innate challenges. Therefore, all relationships we share will be influenced by the curse. Families must grasp this essential truth if we will effectively deal with the opposition.

The Fall of Man and the Curse of God

In Genesis, we learn that God created a perfect family consisting of a sinless man and woman in an unhindered one-flesh union. The first family lived in a perfect world, able to live, multiply, and cultivate the earth in perfect bliss forever. They found complete fulfillment in their relationship with God, and they worshiped him by enjoying his gifts and tasks. Humans were designed for that peaceful fruitfulness: we are wired to live that way. But something broke down badly.

When Adam and Eve sinned by disobeying God, they lost their innocence and disrupted their relationship with their Creator. God had already promised that disobedience would result in death, so death was a foregone consequence of their actions. But as you probably know, neither Adam nor Eve died immediately. Instead, all of Adam's offspring would now be born with a sin nature, at odds with the Creator, destined to eventually die apart from him.

If Adam and Eve's experience of the world had remained unspoiled and perfectly fulfilling, then humankind would have gone on indefinitely without ever sensing their real need—their new need for a *restored* relationship with God. They would have enjoyed the perfect creation and remained blissfully ignorant of their pitiable state until the end of their lives. So God, in his mercy and wisdom, changed the world at that moment into one that would make people restless and discontent with it.

This was actually the good purpose of the curse. The reality of our broken universe would force people to seek spiritual peace and restoration with their Creator, never truly content living apart from him. Furthermore, cursed relationships would prevent people from finding their ultimate happiness in other people. The great blessing of this situation is that people can now—and do!—seek the Lord for their joy and satisfaction and fulfillment. Jesus even then was headed toward the cross to save people from their sin and its consequences.

Of course, even if everyone in your family is saved from their sin, the curse remains in effect. Believers are more equipped to deal with the curse than unbelievers, but we are still prone to the difficulties that arise because of it. The effects of sin will continue to haunt even the godliest of families until Christ returns in his glory. Nevertheless, we can rest in the fact that God has a gracious and loving purpose behind this seemingly harsh punishment. As Bible commentator Henry Morris observed,

> God told Adam that the curse on the ground was *"for thy sake."* It was better that suffering and death accompany sin than that rebellion be permitted to thrive unchecked. . . . And so God placed the curse on man and his whole environment, thus forcing him to recognize the seriousness of his sin, as well as his helplessness to save himself and his dominion from eventual destruction. The necessity of laboring merely to keep alive would go far toward inhibiting further rebellion. . . . Such a condition would encourage him to a state of repentance toward God.[1]

We can take hope, because even in the curse, God intends our good. Understanding God's curse and his purpose behind it helps us anticipate the challenges we will face because of the curse, prepare for them, and restore any damage caused by them.

The Effect of the Curse on Marriage
The curse on the woman and her role in the family is stipulated in Genesis 3:16, an oft-argued verse. There, God told Eve, "I will

surely multiply your pain in childbearing; in pain you shall bring forth children. Your desire shall be for your husband, and he shall rule over you." Those last words—"your desire shall be for your husband, and he shall rule over you"—refer to the drive a wife has to usurp her husband's role and the resulting tension from her husband striving to resist that and dominate her.[2]

This last phrase is enigmatic, but an identical construction in the next chapter of Genesis can help us understand it: God warned Cain about sin because "Its desire is for you, but you must rule over it" (4:7). God meant that sin had an agenda to dominate Cain and that he needed to respond by dominating or overruling sin. Cain's rivalry with temptation parallels, then, the epic battle of the sexes that commenced the moment God spoke that curse to Eve in Genesis 3.

When God cursed Eve, the marriage relationship became innately unfulfilling. No woman could ever be perfectly happy with her husband, lest she never desire a redeeming relationship with her Creator. Likewise, no man would ever be so completed by his wife that he failed to notice the emptiness of the God-shaped vacuum in his own soul. So this part of the curse seems both good and terrible. It is good because it helps us see our need for God and makes us see the futility in making a spouse into an idol: my wife may be a good gift from God, but she can never fulfill me completely, and I will become a despondent tyrant if I demand that of her. But it is terrible because it creates tension between spouses as our desires war within us (James 4:1). The curse is, after all, still a curse.

I should note that because of this particular part of the curse, women have experienced pain in many forms—not only increased pain in bearing children, but also various kinds of physical, mental, and spiritual pain.[3] That is, women have long suffered oppression because men have abused the phrase "rule over her." While we should by no means read that final phrase in Genesis 3:16 as condoning such behavior, we should also assume that God knew how sinners would be tempted to misuse power in their broken world. Indeed, some have done so to horrific effect. The good news is that Jesus came to bear *all* such consequences of the curse.

When people refuse to submit to God's remedy provided in his Word, they will struggle against or under this aspect of the curse, which will bring unhappiness until they turn to God for his mercy. This situation is very good for our eternal well-being, but it poses problems in our marriages. We need to be real about those challenges and humbly seek our God, for we can only face this with courage if we trust God and obey his Word.

The Effect of the Curse on Childbearing

Just as the curse on Eve prevents women from finding ultimate fulfillment in their husbands, so too it prevents them from finding ultimate satisfaction from their children. God begins his curse in Genesis 3:16 by telling Eve, "I will surely multiply your pain in childbearing; in pain you shall bring forth children." There's a reason why many women who have had an epidural during labor say that they wanted to kiss their anesthesiologist. But the point of this verse isn't to highlight the hard work that women go through to bring babies into the world. Instead, it highlights our need for God.

New mothers often experience euphoria after giving birth that makes them forget the *labor* part of labor: the baby they hold in their hands makes it all right. But just wait a few days for the exhaustion to set in, or wait for the baby to enter the terrible twos, and those mothers may suddenly remember those labor pains. This isn't necessarily a bad thing, for families cannot gain full satisfaction from their children. Families must seek God, not trophy children, to enjoy the peace they crave. Only when parents heed God's Word and delight themselves in God rather than in their children can the family experience true fulfillment in childbearing and childrearing.

The Effect of the Curse on Work

Lastly, God cursed the work of the husband. Because Adam obeyed his wife rather than God, "cursed is the ground . . . [and] in pain you shall eat of it all the days of your life" (Genesis 3:17). Men are tasked with providing for their families, but this curse means that no man can ever find a career satisfying, for he cannot truly thrive independent from God's grace. Work will be hard, and it will never be enough: men need their God.

This part of the curse has had a particularly sad effect on families, as men will often try to fill the hollowness they feel with their work. This places devastating strain on wives and children. Work itself is a good thing, but it cannot ultimately satisfy us; when we try to make it do that, we will come up empty every time. But there's a reason why we now have the term "workaholics"—because people often want to work obsessively, seeking more and more recognition through pay, promotion, and pats on the back. The problem is that this desire quenches the thirst for fulfillment the same way seawater does: it seems to fill the space, but it ultimately leaves you parched.

The curse names specific temptations that will interfere with human flourishing, specifically within families: we will be tempted to make our spouses, our children, and our work satisfy us, but none of them can do that. The only way to actually enjoy these things is to realize that they cannot bring us ultimate joy, but God can. This liberates wives and husbands to do what God calls them to do without feeling the pressure to do *more* than God has called them to do. The curse drives us to our point of weakness and need so that we will seek our satisfaction in God himself, not in ourselves or our work or our families. We suffer from intrinsic opposition, and God wants us to realize our insufficiency so that we can rely on his grace for both survival and satisfaction.

Insidious Interference with the Family

In April 2000, scandal rocked the cricket world. It became public that the South African team captain, Hansie Cronje, had on several occasions accepted tens of thousands of dollars from bookies in India to throw international cricket matches. As a result, thirty-year-old Cronje was banned for life from coaching or playing cricket in any capacity. An outspoken Christian, Cronje publically confessed his actions as sin against God, but the damage to the national spirit had already been done. Tragically, two years later, Cronje died in a dramatic plane crash. The nation mourned the sad loss of life, but the pain was complicated because team supporters still felt hurt from the recent betrayal.

Loyal fans can forgive losing streaks, but there is nothing more devastating to morale than finding out that certain individuals threw those games deliberately for personal gain. Fixing matches seems like the epitome of individualism, which is part of the reason why we hate it so much in team sports. We assume that individual team members care more about the success of the team than even their own stats. So too with families, for when individuals in the family prioritize personal agenda over what best serves the family, they undermine the very reason God made them part of a family.

God created us as individuals but brought us together in families, communities, and congregations because we fare better when we work together with others. Members of a family are not solitary individuals: they belong to an integrated system. And that means that personal choices matter to those around you. When you focus on self, everyone suffers, but when you serve your family, everyone wins. As a member of a family, you have the privilege of pursuing God's purpose for you as an individual and for your family as a whole. So watch out for interference that threatens your family unity.

An Inside Job

The fragmentation facilitated by social media and networking technologies pose real challenges to family unity. Facebook, Twitter, texts, emails, and other electronic communication have, like never before, made the world a smaller place. The technological devices that support this phenomenon—smart phones, laptops, tablets— are ubiquitous, connecting more and more people every day. But the platforms and even the devices themselves can create multiple relational barriers within families.

What irony! The very technology that exists to connect people, foster relationships, and facilitate communication has produced an unwitting side effect of disconnecting and isolating people from those closest to them physically and (biblically speaking) relationally. No matter what brand of handheld tools you carry, one little letter drives the whole philosophy of the techno craze today: it's all about *I*, *me*, *my*. And that kind of individualization can destroy a family. Yet we readily adopt the mentality that these devices and apps are unquestionably good and therefore welcome the whole package into the family dynamic. As it turns out, this invasion is an inside job.

Parents regularly use phones, computers, televisions, and other electronic tools in a way that engenders a culture of isolation in the home. We prefer surfing Facebook over talking face-to-face at the dinner table. When kids are old enough to have their own gadgets (the age seems younger every year), parents usher waves of technology into the family. Before we realize it, the waves may drown us.

I'm certainly no technophobe, but we must use these tools wisely and think critically about the social connectivity they apparently facilitate. Technology can be used for good or evil, after all. Because of the pervasive access that even our youngest children have these days to handheld devices, and because of how apparently essential they are becoming to daily life, we must take care how we use them.

If you will possess your gadgets (rather than let your gadgets possess you), you will need to work diligently and maybe take drastic measures. Indeed, Jesus said that we need to get amputative about temptations: "If your eye causes you to sin, tear it out and throw it away" (Matthew 18:9). Not "Poke at your eye a little to make sure it knows you mean business" or even "Pluck it out, but keep it on ice for possible reconstructive surgery later" but "Throw the thing away. And while you're at it, lop off your throwing hand." I'm not suggesting that you trash your computer, television, or mobile phone. But I am saying that you could save your family unity by plucking the selfishness out of your technology (or pulling the "i" off your iPhone!)

Families need to be intentional about how they use communication technology, and they need to acknowledge the biblical priority of their family relationships over friends, acquaintances, and colleagues. Parents should set boundaries conducive to family life and then model these priorities without hypocrisy. Make, adhere to, and enforce rules about phone use and screen time. Teach your kids the difference between *urgent* and *important* (for example, a vibrating phone is urgent, but not important, and homework is important, though perhaps not yet urgent). And school your family in basic courtesy about interrupting live conversations with remote messages. Use electronic tools as *tools*—for benefit, not detriment—and help your children do the same.

Family Unplugged

Every great grunge band has an unplugged album in which they play their classics with plain acoustic instruments. Purists relish the wholesome simplicity of a band that has real skill. So too, there is something healthy about a family that can sit comfortably in each other's company without craving distraction supplied by the outside world.

This realization sank in for me during a visit to a friend's home. My wife and I already admired Jack and Lisa, well known in our ministry circles and even a bit like celebrities to us. So when we received an invitation to their home, we didn't have to check our schedules before we RSVP'd except to clear whatever commitments were inconveniently in the way.

When Kim and I arrived, we were greeted at the door by the couple and, to our surprise, both of their teenage boys. They relayed heartfelt apologies from their daughter, who was working an immovable shift at work, and walked us into a spacious living room lined with books (yes, they still make those) showing signs of use. There was no trace of a television set. The furniture centered around a piano (yes, they still make those) and we sat down to good conversation that included the boys, who asked intelligent questions and contributed informed opinions. The whole family showed genuine affection for one another, and when one son offered to show us his latest organic gardening project, the whole family rose and accompanied us outdoors in a supportive entourage. It was as if they actually enjoyed each other's presence or something. The closest the conversation meandered to the entertainment world was an impromptu piano recital—I kid you not—and a discussion of favorite novels.

By the end of the evening, I could contain my bewilderment no longer, so I asked the parents how they had managed to breed cheerful, compliant teenagers. I felt like I had stumbled upon a magical spring and wanted to take some of the water home with me. Their winning formula was simple: "Family comes first. When the children are alone, they can listen to their music or email friends, but when we are together, they need to be 100 percent here." Both parents modeled this by ignoring mobile phones, which occasionally chirped for attention during dinner. Apparently, texts can go unanswered for a few hours. Interesting.

It's not that this family banished technology from their home. Collectively, the family possessed the full gamut of modern electronic accoutrements, and they used them: the parents had invited us to dinner via email, after all. But the gadgets, like browbeaten serfs, were under the indomitable control of their owners. Even as we sat together, we could see many of their handheld devices casually strewn about the house like powerless paperweights. It seemed clear who was at the beck and call of whom.

Thus, the family guarded their unity not only by shunning disruptive intrusions but also by inextricably involving each other in their individual lives and projects. The family "did life" together. They played their weekly schedule like a team sport. They did not function like a bevy of isolated roommates but supported each other, listened to each other, and respected each other enough to maintain the basic courtesy of ignoring electronic interruptions while in conversation and community with each other.

Baby Steps

Kim and I went home that night resolved to do . . . something. It's not like we articulated seventy resolutions with the eloquence of Jonathan Edwards. We weren't even sure what steps to take, but we knew where we wanted to end up, and we altered our course by degrees wherever we could. We envisioned a future family that would eat together, worship together, and eagerly gather when we summoned everyone at a reasonable decibel level. We wanted a team.

We aimed our first revolt against the tyranny of technology at our family idol: the TV set. I was trapped in the quicksand of habit, having developed an end-of-day routine of coaxing the kids outside to play while I plopped my exhausted carcass down in front of whatever the TV offered while Kim made dinner in our open-plan kitchen. When we built our home, we had two reasons for designing an open kitchen, dining room, and living room: we wanted to easily host large groups for Bible study *and* we wanted to easily see the TV from all spaces. That seems embarrassing to admit now, but it's true. So we knew where to make our first amputation.

Well, we didn't exactly throw away our television; we just moved it to another room because we weren't ready for cold turkey. This was just a baby step. But it was big for us. We also rearranged the furniture to facilitate conversation. Now if we want to watch something on the television, we must move it back into the living room and shift couches out of the way. This actually uses my own laziness as a weapon against itself because where once I watched whatever was there because I felt "too tired" (i.e., lazy and selfish) to do anything productive, I now find myself too lazy to haul out the television, so I play with the kids or chat with my wife while we prepare dinner. Then, in the silence of night while the kids sleep, Kim and I sit on the patio together and read or talk while sipping coffee and snacking on ice cream.

All of these are blessings from God that we almost always snubbed in favor of whatever trivial trash the flat screen proffered. The baby step of putting our television out of sight led to a closer marriage and added small pleasures to the family routine. Soon, conversations with friends were expurgated of all current TV happenings: we can't comment on the latest *American Idol* fiasco or celebrity gossip, not because we have suddenly matured but because we are simply ignorant of current trivia. Oh, blissful ignorance! We now control our television rather than the television controlling us.

Of course, no family will enjoy true unity simply because it has good limits around technology in the home. We should take a lesson here from Jesus' aversion to Pharisaical rules-based religion: you can't legislate family affections anymore than you can legislate love for God. Neither can you make a seventeen-year-old Goth genuinely enjoy the company of a seven-year-old Nintendo addict. But you can show your children the priority of family and face-to-face relationships.

Go to the heart—that is, go to *your* heart. Ask yourself why you want to take your phone to the dinner table with you: is it because you like to feel needed by coworkers or friends? Ask yourself why your family eats so many meals in front of the television: is it because you *cannot* have conversation together? Ask yourself why you will watch *anything* just to have the television on: is it because you fear silence? Ask yourself why you snap at the kids when they walk in front of your football game: is it because you value your leisure time more than their childish curiosities? Ask yourself why you would rather play the latest app than help your spouse cook dinner: is it because you honor your laziness more than your marriage? Maybe you do need to throw out your gadgets, but don't do that without dealing with the heart issue that made you misuse them.

Take small steps if needed, but begin as a family to live day in and day out with a God-centered relationship to technology. What are you willing to forego for a closer family? What are you willing to sever . . . or unplug? Parents, make sure you get your own heart priorities in order before sitting down to talk with your kids about reorienting their relationships to their devices. If you interrupt lecturing your teenager on the value of family, to answer a text, then you slit the throat of the very lesson you are trying to teach. But address this interference to family unity head-on as a family.

You can see behavior change if your understanding changes. That's what this book is all about. If you can comprehend the basics of God's design for the family, the goals of the family, and the positions each member needs to play, you can recalibrate to the pattern God sets in the Bible.

Ask Yourself

1. Because of the curse, we seek fulfillment in our spouses, children, selves, or careers rather than in God. But these good things cannot satisfy us completely; placing ultimate value on them will always end in frustration. Have you noticed intrinsic opposition to success and satisfaction in these areas? That's the curse at work in your everyday life.

   a) How does the curse affect your marriage (e.g., quarrels, role reversal, lack of unity about financial goals)?

   b) How has the curse affected your bearing and rearing of children (e.g., infertility, miscarriages, rebellious children)?

   c) How does the curse affect your workplace (e.g., incompetent boss, faulty products, difficulty reaching goals, unreliable staff)?

2. How have you experienced opposition to God's design from Satan's temptations, worldly philosophies, and your own sinfulness?

   a) What pressures has your family experienced because of how "everybody else is doing it"?

   b) Do any of your family's habits need to be addressed and adjusted (e.g., cellphones at the dinner table, setting family time as a new priority)? Make an action plan for how you could tackle just one such habit.

3. Realizing that the family is God's ordained team unit and that external opposition is real, do you need to ask forgiveness from your spouse or children for treating them as if they are the problem?

Team Basics

Know the Game

Vince Lombardi is hailed as one of the most effective and influential American football coaches in the history of the game—a sentiment established when the NFL's Super Bowl Trophy was renamed in his honor. As head coach of the Greenbay Packers from 1959 to 1967 he never experienced a losing season, starting by being named NFL Coach of the Year in his rookie year and ending with a record 149 wins, 47 losses, and 6 tied games.

How did he do it? One of the secrets to Lombardi's success as a coach was his commitment to continually revisiting the fundamental principles of football. His legendary preseason speech to his team always began with the words, "Gentlemen, this is a football." He would then march his team out to the field and revisit where the end zone was, also pointing out where the out-of-bounds lines were painted. Each season, he would replay these foundations in the minds of his players.

This may have seemed pedantic for great players like the NFL punting yard leader Max McGee, who quipped in reply, "Uh, Coach, could you slow down a little. You're going too fast for us!"[1] But Lombardi's wisdom was continually vindicated on and off the field, and contemporary families have a lot to learn from his training methods.

Back to Basics

Family life is like a team sport—a dynamic network of relationships to manage, goals to accomplish, rules to keep, skills to employ, and strategies to implement. Challenges abound: there are opponents to overcome, injuries to avoid, and obstacles to navigate. And in some cases there are even critics and spectators who observe and evaluate your family's troughs and triumphs.

And just like with team sports, family life can become a chaotic mess when we take the basics for granted. We assume everyone knows the rules of the game, the positions of the players, and the names of the opponents, but maybe they don't. And when we violate the fundamentals of the game, we can experience serious consequences. No matter how many years you have been playing a sport, no matter how accomplished you are in your field, if you break the rules, you suffer penalties. It's the same with the family.

Many families take for granted that every member is committed to the goal and knows what is expected of them. Unfortunately, these days, that assumption is naïve. We must think carefully about the basics of the family dynamic, and then occasionally revisit these fundamentals. By realigning the hearts of each team member with the God who designed the game, we can avert much of the disappointment and frustration of family life. It's no guarantee—even the best teams sometimes lose. But as we saw in chapter 1, families these days tend to get so caught up in the busy techno "whatever" of contemporary life that they forget how God has ordained their family community for a specific purpose . . . if they ever knew it in the first place.

The family is a God-ordained unit—a team. God has assembled your team, and he manages it by revealing his will for the family in Scripture. We might think of the Bible as painting lines on the field: we will suffer consequences for ignoring his rules, because doing so invariably means crossing those lines. No one can play a game with a hodgepodge of teammates who don't know the rules. Neither can you expect your family to function according to God's design if you don't pay attention to God's guidance or understand the positions he tailored to suit each family member.

Some of the foundational premises of family are utterly neglected these days. We may get caught up in the latest strategies and fix-its while forgetting that God long ago laid a clear foundation for the family. Here is a sampling of biblical commands related to the family but frequently called into question, deliberately ignored, or inadvertently neglected:

- God says, "A man shall leave his mother and father and hold fast to his wife" (Genesis 2:24a), but we sometimes say, "The way we always did it in my family growing up was . . ." or "My mom really feels strongly that we should . . ."
- God says that a husband and wife "shall become one flesh" (Genesis 2:24b), but husbands sometimes spend excessive time with "the guys" instead of their wives, or wives want unreasonable amounts of "me time." Tension also arises from the conspicuous absence of joint accounts or shared hobbies. In extreme cases, I have heard of couples planning separate vacations from each other.
- God says, "Husbands, live with your wives in an understanding way" (1 Peter 3:7), but these days, absentee husbands have failed to grasp this most basic of all marriage principles. Between all the man's business trips, fishing excursions, and guys' nights out, he is almost always away from his wife. Even when he's home in body, his mind is lingering at work, his eyes are wired to the TV, or his ears are plugged with ear buds.
- God says, "Husbands, love your wives, as Christ loved the church" (Ephesians 5:25) because the foundation of marriage is sacrificial, selfless, active love. Without this cornerstone, the superstructure totters. But many husbands show more active, selfless sacrifice to their golf foursome than to their families.
- God says, "Wives, submit to your own husbands" (Ephesians 5:22) because it seems pretty basic that no team can have two captains. But when spouses misunderstand the God-

given leadership roles in the family, the design malfunctions, creating a monster with two heads.

- God says, "Children, obey your parents in the Lord" (Ephesians 6:1). Some families have imported the idea of voting from political democracy into the family decision tree, but families where kids outnumber parents can easily appreciate the practical wisdom of God's ordained system of family governance: children need to obey their parents, not the other way around.

- God "has granted to us all things that pertain to life and godliness" (2 Peter 1:3), so Christians should turn instinctively to Scripture for all needed wisdom, but today, we more frequently turn elsewhere. Pop psychology sections in bookstores overflow with marriage advice, unbelievers offer marriage seminars that draw from secular speculation, and moms pluck fortune-cookie wisdom from their baby magazines on how to discipline their kids.

- God says, "Do all to the glory of God" (1 Corinthians 10:31), but we usually think it's unnecessarily radical to take that too seriously. He doesn't really mean *all*, does he? Families that ignore this bedrock foundation stone will misunderstand the goal of marriage and parenting and find themselves unable to define gospel-oriented family success.

To get back to the basics, we must examine what a family is and what it isn't. So get ready for a pep talk on the fundamentals: "Ladies and gentlemen, this is a family . . ."

This Is a Family

Just as if we were looking at a football for the first time, we need to examine the family structure as though it were a foreign concept so that we might simply return to the basics of how the family works. We need to start by investigating what God intended the family to be without rushing to analyze what we experience now. That means we need to study the first (and only) perfect family as described in Genesis 2:18–24.

Leave and Cleave

How do we know that God meant for Adam and Eve to be the model for all future marriages and families? We find the answer at the beginning of Genesis 2:24, when God says, "Therefore a man shall leave his mother and father." This is an odd statement because Adam had no mother or father to leave. We might rightly refer to God as Adam's Father, but that still wouldn't explain why Adam's union with Eve mentions leaving a mother. The word "therefore" is telltale, indicating that God intended this event to somehow serve as the pattern for future events: Adam and Eve's marriage was God's model for all such unions as one man and one woman form a new and distinct, inseparable and permanent family unit. Thus God defined the normal family.

In Genesis 2:18, God saw only one "not good" aspect of creation, and that was the forlorn bachelor. Indeed, any man without the supernatural gift of singleness can attest to how unfeasible sustained singleness is. God solved the problem by creating a companion similar enough to Adam that he considered her "bone of my bone and flesh of my flesh" (2:23), while simultaneously different enough from Adam that she suited him as a helper. The relationship was characterized by profound unity, its members inseparable from each other ("one flesh") yet structurally separate from other families ("leave . . . and cleave"). This is the core of the family's shape: a distinct unit, formed by a man and a woman in an unbreakable bond of oneness, which is recognized and approved by God.

In short, a family is forged when a man and woman commit to live life together and inseparably. Marriage is the nucleus of the nuclear family. Relationships with children (whether biological or adopted), in-laws, grandparents, and any others in or out of the household should be structured around and subservient to the core relationship of the husband/wife team.

The New Normal

To define the family as first and foremost a one-flesh relationship between a husband and wife may sound limited, old-fashioned, or controversial in our contemporary milieu where various cultural factors have obscured this understanding of family. The biblical ideals of lifetime monogamy, heterosexual marriage, and children (which are an important part of many, though not all, biblical families) raised by both mother and father are at least regarded as out-of-date. The more one tampers with the basic makeup of the family unit, the further it departs from God's original design. Suddenly, abnormal becomes the new normal.

We have long regarded divorce as completely normal, and the presence of shared children seems largely irrelevant to a husband's or wife's desire for separation. Parenting magazines regularly claim that a family should center around a child's self-actualization rather than the one-flesh nature of the marriage that began the family. Same-sex couples may now foster and adopt children. Hardly anyone blinks these days at a single woman going to a sperm bank to get the baby she wants. And so on.

We must recognize and accommodate the special circumstances that lead to many of these situations and others like them. Remarriage and the integration of stepsiblings, for example, leads to complex family dynamics that are a real part of contemporary life, and Christians must love people in all family circumstances, looking for opportunities to help those who need help. But acknowledging that there are special cases and accepting responsibility to help them is very different from insisting that we teach those situations to the next generations as appropriate or even preferable to the "old-fashioned" idea of family.

These days, the very definition of marriage makes the news. Lawmakers and lobbyists now weigh in on what constitutes a marriage and a family. That is like polling South African soccer fans about who should play for the Green Bay Packers this season—many of those enthusiasts would have a fundamentally flawed understanding of American football, so their opinions should be taken with a grain of salt, if taken at all. Remember that the "perfect" family of Adam and Eve was short-lived, so now we all suffer from misunderstanding at best. As soon as sin entered the world, their relationship started to strain: Adam and Eve questioned, altered, and disobeyed God's word and then immediately experienced tension and strife. Shame divided the first couple, and Adam tried to shift all the blame to Eve (Genesis 3:12). When human wisdom deviates from God's Word and begins to concoct new ways of doing family, we simply mimic Satan's subtle question, "Has God really said that?" and head toward disaster.

Opinions abound and laws are changed, but God is the one who designed marriage, and he alone defines it. So your family must close ranks against the opposition if you will do what God has made you to do. Start by firmly grasping God's design for the family. Know the game well enough to run for the correct goal lines no matter what chaos surrounds you as you take aim, and understand the challenges that you will face.

Know Your Goal

Roy "Wrong Way" Riegels was almost always a brilliant football player. His coach called him the brightest player in the game. But in the Rose Bowl on New Year's Day of 1929, he made a mistake that haunted him the rest of his life: Riegels somehow spun around as he recovered a fumble and ran full speed for 69 yards in the wrong direction. The radio commentator Graham McNamee spoke what was on everyone's mind as Riegels charged the opposite end zone: "What am I seeing? What's wrong with me? Am I crazy? Am I crazy? Am I crazy?"

It was one of the most memorable moments in football history, and one Riegels would never live down. To his credit, he took the field to play the second half of the game and played his heart out. But his mistake has become a classic illustration for the importance of knowing where you're headed. So we see that many families today are charging ahead . . . but toward what end? Are they shaping family life according to God's direction?

To Glorify God Together

If someone asked you or your spouse what the goal of your family is, what would you say? In whatever season you find your family (with or without children in the home), you as a couple should contemplate your "family mission." A marriage that coasts with no deliberate direction will circle haphazardly like a preschool soccer team. Your family should not necessarily look like others that you see. All individuals are unique, and that means all families are unique, so they should not all act the same way. The "normal" family is not one that upholds some particular standard of behavior but one that reflects God's design in structure and function.

Defining your particular family mission must start with understanding God's ultimate goal for the family—the object of the game, as it were. So you have left your father and mother and cleaved to your spouse . . . then what? If you ask most people about their goal in life or even in marriage, they would probably say, "To be happy." But what is the object of the Christian life? What, in fact, is the object of all human existence?

The well-known Westminster Confession opens with this question and answer: "What is the chief end of man? To glorify God and enjoy him forever." We might replace "man" with any object or entity: "What is the purpose of your TV or company or vegetable garden or indoor soccer league? Why does it exist?" If the answer isn't a sincere "to glorify God and enjoy him," then there is something profoundly pointless about your pursuit. Glory and enjoyment ride in tandem for Christians. Human beings were created for fellowship with God, and we are most fulfilled in our lives, relationships, and endeavors when we pursue them as a means of glorifying and fellowshiping with God.

So why does *your* family exist? What is its chief end? If your answer isn't essentially, "To glorify God and enjoy him forever," then your family is missing its point. To begin realigning, I suggest that you write out God-centered goals for your family. Just as schools have mottos and business have mission statements, families need a *raison d'etre*, or a reason for being. But remember that you shouldn't just make one up: root the goal for your family in God's ultimate reason for families. God gave you a spouse, and perhaps children (whether now or in the future), and all other relationships for one primary reason: to bring him glory.

To Enjoy Him Together

Husband, you must lead in this. Emulate Joshua's bold and definitive example when he declared to the nation of Israel, "Choose this day whom you will serve. . . . But as for me and my house, we will serve the Lord" (Joshua 24:15). Husband, ask God for wisdom about how exactly your household should "serve the Lord." What will that look like for your specific family? Share your understanding with your wife and ask her what she thinks too. Seek a unified sense of purpose for your family, and make a plan with your wife as to some practical steps you might take together toward that goal.

If you have children, it is up to you as the parents to know and communicate your family's goals regularly and succinctly so that they might be embedded in the hearts of your children. Moses set this mandate before Israelite parents as they prepared to enter the promised land: they needed to love and obey God, and they needed to constantly impart that example of love and obedience to their families in the warp and woof of daily living.

> Hear, O Israel: The LORD our God, the LORD is one. You shall love the LORD your God with all your heart and with all your soul and with all your might. And these words that I command you today shall be on your heart. *You shall teach them diligently to your children*, and shall talk of them when you sit in your house, and when you walk by the way, and when you lie down, and when you rise.
>
> —Deuteronomy 6:4–7

When we adhere to God's plan and purpose for the family, God is glorified and we enjoy the rich blessings that come from obeying him. If you hope that your family exists to make your life easy or to make you happy, then you will get disillusioned with family life. If you just sit back and chill, figuring that a family coasting along in the world will work well enough for you—that your marriage is good enough and that the goals parents commonly set for their children in the world will do just fine—your family may end up heading in the opposite direction from where God wants you to be. You may chase your goals with gusto, but if you have not set your eyes on God's goals, you are in danger of duplicating Wrong Way Riegels's mistake.

Define your goals according to God's original design for the family and his specific calling for your family. Then you can work together as a team, depending upon the Holy Spirit to energize and bless that work. You can also judge your successes or failures according to God's standards rather than according to human wisdom, which may change with every generation. You can even enjoy the work of glorifying God as a part of the family team, receiving the blessings that come from belonging to and participating in a God-glorifying family.

Prepare Your Defense

As any athlete knows, reaching the goal line isn't as simple as just running for it; a game gets exciting when the defense poses a legitimate challenge as a worthy opponent. The family team encounters opposition as well, but it does not generally make real life fun or exciting: instead, it makes life hard, and we need to respond with unified and strategic defense for the sake of the family. I have seen families fall apart during challenging seasons because they fail to view each family member as part of the team. In the fog of tension, they may even target each other, and the defense falls apart. We must address any serious challenge that comes from within or without quickly and directly as an attack on family unity, lest it become a wedge within the family.

After Adam and Eve's initial plunge into sin, the first family suffered marital tension, then a deadly feud. Genesis 4 shows Cain and Abel at odds simply because of sin. Cain became recalcitrant because God rejected his substandard offering (verse 5), and his sullen dejection turned into anger, malice, and envy. He lashed out at his brother who had done nothing more than obey God. In the end, Cain's vindictiveness culminated in cold-blooded murder. When God asked Cain about Abel's whereabouts, Cain's response in verse 9 betrayed the problematic attitude lurking in his heart: "Am I my brother's keeper?"

Obviously, Cain thinks the answer is "No," but that means he does not understand how relationships within a family work. Should we act as guardians for our family members? Should we care about their well-being at all times? Absolutely. But the sin of disregard and even murderous hatred crouches at the door of our heart, tempting us to believe that we are not responsible for one another. We fail to defend the family appropriately against challenges because we think we don't need to do so. Sin therefore drives a wedge between us, poisoning our loyalty and turning us against our relatives. Sin makes us like malignant cancer in the family unit, consuming our own flesh and blood to the destruction of the whole body.

We should not regard as "normal" any kind of rivalry between siblings or other family members. Christians must take Paul's admonition to the Philippian church to heart, especially within the bonds of family:

> Do nothing from selfish ambition or conceit, but in humility count others more significant than yourselves. Let each of you look not only to his own interests, but also to the interests of others.
>
> —Philippians 2:3–4

I do not mean to suggest that we must put an end to all friendly jostling, especially among children. But there is a marked difference between healthy competition and vindictive one-upmanship. In the sport of fencing, opponents salute before they duel and shake hands afterwards as signs of honor. So too, we must temper all competition within the family with respect or the tension will turn toxic and morph into malevolence. When love binds a husband and wife or brothers and sisters, competition can be edifying. But where latent envy or bitterness lurk in the heart, betrayal and conflict is crouching at the door.

The primary definition of the family is the husband and wife as "one flesh," and opposition to every family will begin there—disrupting the basic unity of the family. Every member of the family is responsible for family unity, and that unity is essential to face every challenge you will face. Families need to learn to see each other as teammates, not opposed to one another but together on the same side of whatever conflicts they face. Even when the family suffers disagreements or disappointments, you must learn to view the issue objectively and return to the basics if the conflict threatens family unity. Regularly practice the mindset of brotherly love that the apostle Peter enjoined churches to cultivate:

> Finally, all of you, have unity of mind, sympathy, brotherly love, a tender heart, and a humble mind. Do not repay evil for evil or reviling for reviling, but on the contrary, bless, for to this you were called, that you may obtain a blessing.
>
> —1 Peter 3:8–9

A united family brings untold blessings, just as unchecked contention brings damaging consequences. But each family member must know and play his or her own unique position as well as respect the function of the other players. This is how the family will flourish. As Coach Lombardi once said, "The achievements of an organization are the results of the combined effort of each individual." So when you see a family united for God's glory, no one family member can take the credit, for the individuals have together depended upon grace for the good of their family.

Ask Yourself

We encounter many family difficulties due to our ignorance of the Scriptures, which show us God's design for the family.

1. Think about whether you need to make a plan to reacquaint yourself and your family with God's design for each person's role. Where are you strong as a family? Where are you weak?

2. Plan a time or several times for your family to gather and read the passages mentioned in this chapter, especially the foundational principles under the heading "Back to Basics." Talk together—spouses first, and then parents with children—about what God says about families and ask him to reorient your family to his design.

3. Each family member who is old enough should identify how he or she sometimes behaves in ways that are inappropriate based on what God says their role should be. Spouses, make action plans together about how you might repent and grow in grace. Parents, make specific plans with your children for how you might help them play their positions well.

3

Team Captain

Dad, Play Your Position

The flamboyant Columbian national soccer team's goalkeeper René Higuita was renowned for his on-field eccentricities. He was especially famous for the spectacular and photogenic "scorpion kick" that became legendary. Higuita would jump high off the ground and flip horizontally, blocking the ball from going over his head by bringing his legs up like a scorpion tail. Truly prodigious. And it worked: Higuita is regarded as one of the best all-time South American goalkeepers.

But this goalkeeper was also notorious for coming far out from his goals. At times, Higuita would dribble the ball as far as the center of the field, leaving his nervous defenders to keep the goals even though they were limited in doing that. Higuita is credited with scoring three goals in sixty-eight international matches, which simply isn't normal behavior for a goalkeeper. Perhaps that's why his nickname was "El Loco," or "The Madman."

It seemed that flaunting the conventions of his position would eventually lead to disaster. Sure enough, in Columbia's 1990 World Cup "round of 16" game against Cameroon, Higuita was near the halfway line when an opposing striker stole the ball from him and took it all they way to score a winning goal in a keeperless net, costing Colombia their shot at the World Cup title.

When God invented the family, he gave the man the role of leader and protector like the goalkeeper on a soccer team, but many husbands and fathers have moved out of their assigned positions to disastrous effect. Men, understanding God's design will help you understand who you are in your family, the larger society, and the kingdom of God. And submitting to God's design will help you actually become what you are designed to be.

The Leader as Head

In Genesis 2, God told Adam to name the animals and then, when Eve was brought to him, he named her too. Chauvinists who know enough Bible to be dangerous like to point out that naming signaled authority, as though this somehow teaches that husbands own their wives. But the main point of federal headship—or true authority, for that matter—is responsibility.

This term "federal headship" may sound enigmatic to you, but you probably understand it better than you think. In football, why do they fire the head coach the week after a team loses the state championship? The coach didn't fumble the ball, miss a play, or get sent off for fighting. But he's responsible for the team's performance. Or when a rambunctious five-year-old gleefully pulls cans of tuna off the shelf in the grocery store just to hear the repeated plunks on the floor, the manager walks past the offending kid and approaches the parent. We understand headship.

This is a biblical reality as well. Who listened to the serpent in Genesis 3? Eve. Who took the fruit? Eve. Who ate the fruit? Eve. Who gave the fruit to her husband? Eve. But whom did God summon? Adam. Wait. What? I think I would have responded with finger-pointing exactly as Adam did: "The woman you gave me, she did it!" The weak link in this mixed doubles team seemed to be Eve, yet God held Adam primarily responsible. Why? Because the husband is the head of the family. Even when a husband doesn't act like the head, he is still the head, and God holds him responsible for the team.

God put Adam in charge of leading and protecting his wife, so when his wife plunged the human race into irreversible condemnation, God took the husband to the woodshed for a chat. Perhaps this seems unfair to you, but it is no more or less fair than Jesus taking responsibility for your sin. As the second Adam, Jesus answered for our sin and took its consequences on our behalf. This is the way God's world works. Though you may not function that way in your home, God will still call the husband to account for his leadership (or lack thereof).

Paul clearly teaches this kind of headship in Ephesians 5:23 and 1 Timothy 2:12–14. So if you are a single guy reading this right now, you should take note: don't marry a woman you can't lead. It doesn't matter how much you like her personality, her looks, or her interests; your job is to lead her, not stare at her. Christians aren't called to political correctness but biblical living, and if this is how God the Creator wants the family to operate, then who are we to accommodate opposing sensibilities? We are but creatures, designed to bear God's image in the world exactly as he commands us to do so.

What does it mean to lead? Headship does not entitle husbands to bark commands but obligates them to tremendous responsibility. First on the "to do" list is study: if you will "live with your [wife] in an understanding manner" (1 Peter 3:7), you must pursue a PhD in your wife. And this means a lifetime as student, because just when you think you've got her all figured out, she changes. Wife-ology, like astronomy, is a field of research that you never really get a grasp on because the possibilities for research never end. And like astronomy, wife-ology leads to discoveries of the most breathtaking beauty as well as the most terrifying threats. But a husband's concerns are more pressing than the potential discovery of life on other planets: his wife deserves intimate study and care.

The Leader as Provider

Some men behave like they take their cues from lions. Male lions contribute little to meal preparation, lazing around all day while the lionesses hunt. The females in the pride coordinate a kill, exert tremendous energy in the chase, do the dirty work of killing the prey, and then back off until the male lopes in and takes the lion's share, as it were. The exhausted females wait patiently for their head to finish his third helping before they pick at whatever he leaves. This should not be so in the Christian family.

In the Bible, God elevates the woman's role to one of honor. And a husband has a responsibility to provide for his wife. This is so fundamental to society that Paul speaks of it as an axiom that even unbelievers understand (1 Timothy 5:8). What about wives who work? We will discuss this hot topic in the next chapter. Here, we must understand that the scriptural principle is this: when there is a man in the family, it is his primary responsibility to provide for the needs of his entire household. We most commonly see this provision worked out through a combination of his earned income and the shared stewardship of spending that income. But the point here is that the primary responsibility for provision lies with the husband, not the wife.

Men who unnecessarily pressure their wives into shouldering part of the income burden are not behaving as true men. According to Paul, they are not even behaving as Christians. The woman's curse is the increased pain of bearing children, and the man's curse is the sweaty personal work of earning bread for his family. Work is good, and God gave people work to do before the fall, but after the fall, that good work became hard, and men and women had different curses to bear. No man can birth children, so no man can really help a woman bear her part of the curse. When a husband forces his wife to work, he leeches assistance from her in the hard work that is his to do.

Of course, there is more to provision than how much one earns. Part of leading the family means guarding against poor spending habits. Wealth comes from spending less than you earn. No matter what you earn, if your family consumes more than you make, you will end up broke: "The soul of the sluggard craves and gets nothing, while the soul of the diligent is richly supplied" (Proverbs 13:4). Many people believe that making more money will solve their financial problems, but that is not how money works. Take a lesson from the wisest, richest man who ever felt depressed: King Solomon warned that "He who loves money will not be satisfied with money, nor he who loves wealth with his income (Ecclesiastes 5:10).

Part of being a good provider, then, is learning to save, invest, and spend wisely. Put another way, avoid foolish debt (see Proverbs 13:7). Some say that Christians should stay completely out of debt, but the Bible does not speak specifically to credit cards or mortgages, so we must think carefully about the difference between sinful debt and wise leverage. It's not debt if you can clear it instantly: if I borrow ten dollars for lunch, I'm good for it, but if I borrow a million bucks, I become a slave to my debt (Proverbs 22:7). With a substantial deposit on a house, you can sell quickly even at reduced cost if needed. Similarly, a decent deposit on a car can keep you from getting upside down on the loan and simple repossession will free you of debt. These aren't good situations, but they do erase the debt. Credit cards from clothing stores are more complicated, though: if you end up unable to pay, you can't return the worn clothes. When you finance lifestyle, experience, or liabilities instead of assets, you run great risk.

Contentment is the key. Are you, as a husband, paying attention to the real needs of your family and working your hardest to graciously provide for them? If you still cannot make ends meet, seek counsel from godly men and women around you about how better to manage your income or to perhaps pursue additional income. But take a step back when your kids complain. Maybe their temporary unhappiness doesn't actually mean that you need to work harder to provide more. Maybe you need to work on teaching them contentment instead.

The Leader as Protector

South Africa holds the world's carjacking record with a whopping 16,000 cases per year, nearly eighteen times more than anywhere else. Hijacking has reached such epidemic proportions that there are now road signs warning motorists of the crime's hotspots. In 1998 the inventive pyromaniac Charl Fourie marketed a liquid petroleum spray that functioned as a flamethrower for cars: if some-one unwanted approached your car while you were in it, you could activate the flamethrower and set their legs ablaze. Male drivers particularly found this product alluring, and Fourie's first customer was the Johannesburg police superintendent. But reason prevailed in the court system, and the invention was outlawed.

Yes, there is something in a man that wants to ward off bad guys. There are biblically masculine ways to enact such protection, and then there are culturally enmeshed macho ways to do it. As cool as it would be to own a flamethrower, that's probably not the best way for a husband to make sure that he protects his family.

Physical Protection

When Paul wrote that "no one ever hated his own flesh, but nourishes and cherishes it" (Ephesians 5:29), he had both provision and protection in mind. Husband, if your body is hungry, you feed it. When it's cold, you put a coat on it. When it's stressed, you take it on vacation. Paul says that your wife and family are part of your body, so your instinct to self-protection must automatically cover them too.

My wife and I take shifts getting up at night for a crying baby, but there is one duty that is always my job: "bump in the night" duty. Living in South Africa, where the burglary rate is high, you don't ignore a sound in your house at night. I possess no ability or proclivity for hand-to-hand combat, but if my wife and kids are going to experience physical harm from an intruder, it will have to be over my dead body. So too whether you live in a place with high or low crime rates, it is the husband's responsibility to get between his family and danger. Churches need not teach kung fu in their men's classes, but they should cultivate an attitude of chivalry and a disposition toward protection.

Most of the time, a husband's duty to protect his family is far from dramatic: he must simply do what he can to ensure a physically safe environment. Put up a fence to keep toddlers away from the swimming pool and out of traffic, make sure the dog has its shots and is friendly enough to let kids poke it in the eye, give lessons on how to hold a pair of scissors, make rules about the garbage disposal: these are all ways dad needs to be on top of home safety. We often see hygiene, inoculations, and road sense as the wife's role, but God will hold the husband primarily responsible for physical hurts suffered by those under his care.

This means that dads need to think carefully about who drives your kids around and who babysits them. Statistically, physical and sexual abuse of children happens more from people they know than people they don't. Dads, be involved. Make sure you have good insurance, medical care, and a safe car, but take a broad view of protection for your family. These are not strictly Christian duties, but a godly dad needs to be involved in creating and maintaining an environment that keeps his family safe from harm and secure from attack.

Emotional Protection

A wise husband tends to stay out of conflicts between his wife and her mother. Like a boxing referee, he is safer dancing around the conflict than trying to get between the fighters. But some mother-daughter relationships can be quite toxic and unedifying, so a caring husband must put himself in harm's way to absorb the brunt of incoming pain and speak healing words (Proverbs 12:18).

You would get in the way of an intruder brandishing a knife blade, right? Words can be just as devastating to your wife, especially coming from a person she loves, like her friends or her mom. A wife frequently in tears because of a verbally abusive friendship or other mean-spirited acquaintance needs her husband to step in and say, "Enough." Even where the issues are complex and fraught with decades of sinful patterns, a husband has the right and responsibility to get involved in protecting his wife's emotional well-being if and when he can.

Fathers must do similar work for their children, especially for their daughters. In this day of serial dating, girls often find their hearts repeatedly trampled by a long line of losers. Train your sons to guard the hearts of their friends, particularly those of the opposite sex, and train your daughters in bold purity. You must also train your children to keep good friends (1 Corinthians 15:33).

Be involved from the first day, Dad, and then don't back off. You may spend the first sixteen years of parenting protecting your children's morals, and then, because "everybody's doing it," you abdicate your role by sending them into a wolf pack of hormonal teenagers. Do not assume that your daughter is strong enough to withstand boys with slick tongues and manipulative moves aimed at getting her to think she's enough in love to offer herself up. And do not assume that your son is strong enough to withstand peer pressure and cultural messages that objectify women. I do not advocate a particular method of courting (as a father of a girl, my new personal favorite is arranged marriage!), but dads must be on guard for their daughters' emotions and their sons' attitudes. Emotions are the thread with which boys unravel girls' self-control.

Spiritual Protection

Spiritual protection does not simply mean forbidding your kids to read certain books or watch certain movies. There is far more to guard than just the family library. Take a lesson from John Bunyan's lesser-known allegory *The Holy War*, which describes the enemy Diabolo's medieval attack on the city of Mansoul. Diabolo levels this attack at the five gates, which represent the five senses, and he reserves the most violent assault for the eye-gate. Dad needs to take the responsibility of fortifying his family's eye-gates, which includes supervising input from television, magazines, and the Internet. He also needs to watch the ear-gate, through which we pump unbiblical philosophy in the form of popular songs.

Even so, spiritual protection does not consist of merely guarding the gates from what is harmful. It also means actively encouraging what is profitable. Husbands, don't just think about what your wife reads as "woman" stuff—encourage deep theology and rich stories, and read with her even if you don't think of yourself as a reader. Dads, get involved in what your children watch, read, listen to, and scroll past so fast on social networking sites, but don't just forbid what would harm them: protect them spiritually by helping them understand and enjoy rich truth and beautiful art.

Godly dads also protect their children spiritually by preparing them for the future. Most parents provide simple shields, guarding them from foolish decisions while they are children, but you also must prepare your children to make good decisions when they are grown. Train them in godly disciplines that will serve them well all the days of their lives, and shape them with a biblical worldview.

- *Spiritual disciplines.* Teach your children habits of private devotions, making sure they actually listen to sermons, learn (through example) how to serve the church, contribute financially to God's kingdom, and pray. Even dads without theological training should get involved in training their kids to interpret the Bible, evangelize the lost, and articulate their theological positions. Children getting ready to leave home should be able to recognize false teaching and answer common atheistic arguments.

- *Worldview training.* Do you know how school, television shows, and peers affect your kids' opinions, attitudes, and convictions? Prepare your children to think well, make wise decisions informed by God's Word, and defend their views. But don't raise Pharisees who can regurgitate the "right" answers from hard hearts. Instead, understand your children so that you can shepherd them biblically (Proverbs 20:5). As they grow, discuss culturally relevant topics with direct questions about abortion, euthanasia, same-sex marriage, military draft, tattoos, popular music, physical beauty, the depiction of women in advertising, and sex outside of marriage. Dad, you should model humble, civil, biblically informed dialogue for your children.

It is not the church's job to guard your children and prepare them for life. Rather, God appoints a dad as leader of every family's defense department. Make no mistake: the head of the family bears the ultimate responsibility here. A dad who does not take seriously his children's spiritual upbringing will reap the consequences later (Proverbs 22:6). Take a broad view of your duty to spiritually protect your family.

The Leader as Cultivator

"Pimp My Ride" is a ridiculous TV show, but most men I know love watching the mechanics take some beat-up car and make it turn heads with low-riding suspension, purple flame decals, velvet seats, video screens, a fridge, a computer, and more bass speakers than they have at a U2 concert. I've seen guys get inspired to do the same to their VWs. The bass on our street can rattle windows and neutralize pacemakers. Why? Because men like to upgrade.

This is actually biblical. (Not the bass—that's from somewhere else.) Adam, after all, was created to *tend* the garden. God gave him this sphere of influence and responsibility, and it also served as a channel for worship. God could have created a garden that self-mowed, self-pruned, and auto-arranged itself with the flick of a refresh button, like when the icons on your desktop clip into place with the click of a mouse. But he didn't. God created a world that needed men and women to keep it, cultivate it, and tend it. This was a pre-fall job description. All the curse did was make the work harder—more urgent, and less satisfying—particularly for men.

But this God-given drive to cultivate made men build farms, civilizations, and even empires. Sometimes the need to upgrade appears as sinful chest-pounding machismo, but at its core, this desire to upgrade reflects God's design for human beings and specifically for men. Animals don't build roads or set up educational systems for their offspring. They don't explore the savanna beyond where the next berry comes from. Improvement and cultivation is a human trait, reflecting God's creative design of us as image bearers.

Satan can't stop this drive, but he sometimes redirects it into entertainment cul-de-sacs. Young men often find themselves tempted to postpone real adulthood, never learning how to take care of house and family but spending hours playing video games and working out. They may not be acting like men, but they feel like it when they get promoted to new gaming levels. Or think about a dad with out-of-control kids, an emotionally distant wife and a lackluster job, who doesn't worry about leading his family toward unity and joy but feels like a man because his handicap has finally dropped a stroke on the golf course. Some men merely live vicariously through multiple leisure activities.

But men were made to *make*—to cultivate what God has created for the benefit of others, and specifically to provide for and protect the family God has given them. Any contribution you make to your family and your larger society through your field of work deserves more praise than whatever successes you might achieve outside of those realms. So "Look carefully then how you walk, not as unwise but as wise, making the best use of the time, because the days are evil. Therefore do not be foolish, but understand what the will of the Lord is" (Ephesians 5:15–17).

No Quick Fix

Remember goalkeeper René Higuita? Remember how he flubbed Columbia's 1990 World Cup game by moving out of position? It's a wonder that he survived that error: Columbian soccer players have been killed for less. Even Higuita recognized that he made a poor decision at the end of that game, calling it "a mistake as big as a house."

What happens when Christian husbands and dads move out of their God-given position as protector and leader of the family? Christians are known for taking family seriously (maybe not as seriously as Columbia takes soccer, but still). Yet does anyone do anything about family goalkeepers who come way out of their goals? I'm not at all suggesting assassination, but some sort of confrontation would be appropriate.

When was the last time you heard of church discipline for a dad spending too little time with his family? We tend to take sins with immediate effects more seriously, but absentee fathers cause long-term suffering. When kids "go off the rails" in their late teens, the church commiserates with the weepy parents; that's not the time or place to lash a dad for years of sowing what he now reaps. But there was a time and place: it was eighteen years before when the baby came home and dad began making a series of tiny decisions reflected in phrases like "That's woman's work" or "I've got a job to do and don't have paternity leave." Those patterns and habits form character that cannot be changed overnight.

Sometimes, when a dad sits in my office crying about his teen's latest debacle, asking me for a biblical solution, I have to resist the temptation to recommend time travel. Going back eighteen years and starting over may seem like the only thing to do. The second best option is to repent and start doing the right thing now, and that can prove equally difficult.

What does that kind of repentance look like? It's not about learning techniques but about developing character that can only be forged in the furnace of godly living day-in and day-out. Men tend to want to fix things (except the light in the refrigerator): tell me how to be a great dad and I'll schedule it and get it done. But that's not how fatherhood works. Dads need to *become* what God wants them to *be*, not just *do* what they need to *do*. To be honest, many men I have known need a complete overhaul of the soul to become the husbands and fathers God wants them to be. And if you're in that category, you need to go back to the Bible and start from scratch. Reformat the hard drive of your social norms and reinstall the new operating system found only in God's Word.

Lazy, distracted, misdirected machismo is the scourge of young manhood. Stop playing video games or golf and watching TV. Instead, go fix your roof, actively parent your children, contribute to society, and upgrade your world. Get involved in your church. Ask your wife for a honey-do list rather than groaning when she suggests one. Buy her something small and unexpected to show that you know her, take your family on vacation, and keep asking, "What's next?" All of which is to say . . . men, remember the creation mandate of Genesis 2, and play your position.

Ask Yourself

Husbands and fathers need to realize that God has given them an important assignment on the home team: you bear the responsibility to lead your wives and children spiritually, to provide for your families financially, to protect them in various ways, and to steward your possessions and sphere of influence. But that list isn't meant to send you on a guilt trip: you have all that you need in Christ to fulfill your role.

1. Is there any portion of your God-given role that you consistently neglect? Ask God to humble you so that you might see your strengths and weaknesses clearly. You might also ask your wife for some insight: if you do, prepare to listen and prayerfully consider what she says without rushing to defend yourself!

2. Where needed, ask forgiveness of anyone affected by your neglect, and set goals to improve. Enlist the help of your wife to identify what needs to take highest priority, and begin to work on that first.

3. If your wife has been leading in the areas you are meant to (e.g., she has been doing family devotions while you watch football), then ask her forgiveness and step up to the plate. Your family may bump through this transition, and you may need to remind your wife and children how God's Word makes clear that you should actively lead the family. Do not hesitate even in the same breath to repeat how you realize that you had been neglecting your role. Remember that leaders are always first to serve, choosing to become the least and the lowest wherever possible. And continue to ask your wife how you can better play your biblical position: she is your helpmeet even in this! (In case you haven't figured it out yet, this assignment is best enjoyed with a generous portion of humble pie.)

4

Team MVP

Leader in Assists

My first year out of college, I taught English and coached basketball in a South African high school. Basketball was new to South African public schools, where cricket, field hockey, netball, and rugby are the staple sports, but some students petitioned the school that year to start a basketball team. All they needed was a coach. No other faculty member had ever even played a casual game of pick-up basketball, so I volunteered even though I was rather unqualified.

During our first practice, I noticed that some of the kids could regularly make difficult shots. Michael Jordan had led the NBA for several seasons then as the highest scorer, and they all wanted to be like Mike, so they practiced shooting for hours in their backyards. But a gaggle of Michael Jordan clones doesn't make a good basketball team. They didn't know how to pass the ball or work together. In fact, they had zero strategy beyond "whoever has the ball takes a shot at the basket." They were their own opponents, rivaling each other for opportunity to show off their dunking skills.

It became apparent that I needed to disabuse these zealous wannabes of the idea that the team's most valuable player was the one who could make baskets. They needed to learn how to identify the real MVP. They needed a new hero.

Enter Magic Johnson, the renowned point guard of the Los Angeles Lakers. Johnson earned the NBA Finals MVP award in his rookie year, but that was just the start. He secured the NBA MVP award three times in his career and the All-Star MVP award twice.

He also led the league in regular season assists four times and remains the NBA's all-time leader in average assists per game.

The point guard is essential to a successful basketball team, but the measure of a great point guard isn't in the number of baskets made—it's in the number of assists. The point guard plays a specialized role running the team's offense by ensuring that the ball gets to the right players at the right time. He or she must perfectly grasp and accept the coach's game plan in order to control the ball and execute that plan during play. The point guard rarely scores points but instead helps others do so. That's an "assist"—when a player passes the ball to a teammate in a way that makes it possible to score.

The assist is the real magic of basketball. That's what made Magic Johnson so invaluable: his consistent ability to help other people score. Every family needs someone with the same skill.

Bring on the Magic

When God designed the family, he made the woman a kind of point guard who assists her team in reaching its full potential: she is the "helper" in God's family blueprint (Genesis 2:18). That sounds like a lesser role to most folks these days, at least when it comes to the family, and our families are suffering because of it—just like a basketball team suffers when all its players want to be little Michael Jordans and no one knows anything about Magic Johnson. We need our families to bring on the Magic . . . which may mean that we need to rethink the roles of men and women.

It has been well established that women can do what men do, and sometimes much better. The question here, however, is not what a person *can* do, but what a person *should* do to accomplish God's game plan for the family. It is a question of role or function, not comparative value, though we are keen to make it seem that way.

> If I set the sun beside the moon,
> And if I set the land beside the sea,
> And if I set the town beside the country,

And if I set the man beside the woman,
I suppose some fool would talk about one being better.
             —G. K. Chesterton, "Comparisons"

A wife is God's gift to help her husband accomplish their God-given responsibilities: the helper made especially for him (Genesis 2:18–23). She is not there to take over any of his workload, on top (or instead) of hers, to make things easier for him. Neither is she there to operate as a household servant. Rather, the wife has the God-given responsibility to manage the home in a way that assists her husband in their shared dominion over the creation and in his particular battle for the family's bread.

Adam, after all, could not do the work God gave him to do by himself. He was inadequate, or incomplete, without Eve. We see this in Genesis 2, where God describes the one deficiency in his new creation along with his remedy: the bachelor was a prize specimen, but he was designed to need help (Genesis 2:18). Adam then readily admitted his neediness when he beheld his new bride and delivered the very first gushing "you complete me" speech (2:23).

When Adam saw Eve, he knew that she was exactly the "help" he needed. Eve was stunningly different from any other creature Adam had seen. While obviously very much like him (he immediately recognized her as "flesh of my flesh"), she was unmistakably unique. The animals could not do the job, and note that God did not make another man for Adam to merely befriend or cultivate the garden alongside. Far from needing assistance with his work, Adam suffered from a systemic inadequacy and required customized, complementary companionship.

God therefore made the woman to meet the very need God had programmed into the man. She is called a "helpmeet suitable" in the Hebrew (Genesis 2:18, 20) because God designed her to suit her husband emotionally, spiritually, and even physically. The husband and wife truly complement one another: the husband supports and delights in his wife even as the wife helps her husband become all God intends for him to be. Romantic feelings, spiritual connection, and physical attraction are all part of God's design for this new "one flesh" union.

The "S" Word

George Bernard Shaw once made the wry observation that "England and America are two countries separated by a common language." So too my wife and I, for she hails from California whereas I was born in a British colony. We make it work, but not without some comical moments. With her patient help, I have learned to navigate around the common interpretive landmines. For example, what Brits call a *pancake*, Americans call a *crépe*, and what the Americans deem a *pancake*, their counterparts across the pond call a *crumpet*. I now know that on American soil, what I think of as a *biscuit* is a *cookie*, though American biscuits are, fortunately, just as delectable, if meant to be smothered in gravy rather than dipped in tea.

As you can see, our words often have different connotations depending on our cultural setting. I have found this true not only about food but also about scriptural terms. So when I preach on the subject of submission, a congregation's reaction depends not on what God's Word says but on what they think when they hear the word. Sometimes, we need translation assistance—scriptural subtitles, if you like. Let's take a closer look, then.

When Paul and Peter wrote that Christian wives should submit to their own husbands, they used the Greek word *hupotasso*, which means to arrange in proper order. The first part of the word (*hupo*) means *under*, as in the English word *hypoglycemic*, meaning low blood sugar. The second part (*tasso*) is distantly related to the English word *tag*, like when you tag or label boxes in a move so that everything goes to its proper place in the new house. Every item in the universe has a tag—a God-given label for the position it should occupy, or the proper role it should play in giving God glory. The task of the Christian is to identify his or her own tag, or place, in God's ordained structure, and then function in that position to God's glory.

Some people misunderstand God's assignments and become disgruntled or envious of others. Paul refers to this thinking in 1 Corinthians where he shows the folly of a church member craving the spiritual gift of another member:

> The body does not consist of one member but of many. If the foot should say, "Because I am not a hand, I do not belong to the body," that would not make it any less a part of the body. And if the ear should say, "Because I am not an eye, I do not belong to the body," that would not make it any less a part of the body. If the whole body were an eye, where would be the sense of hearing? If the whole body were an ear, where would be the sense of smell? But as it is, God arranged the members in the body, each one of them, as he chose. If all were a single member, where would the body be?
>
> —1 Corinthians 12:14–19

Just as each part of the body must do what it was designed to do, each of us must play our assigned positions—this is a way of worshiping God! To balk against his wisdom is unwise and leads to dysfunction and trouble.

No one is immune from the need to submit. Jesus submitted to the Father (John 12:49), and Christians should submit to their church leaders (Hebrews 13:17). God administers his sovereign authority through fallible, sinful human authorities (is there another kind?) and commands us to respect them (see Romans 13:1–2 and 1 Peter 2:18). We might take as an object lesson those angels who refused to submit and who therefore did not keep their proper position of authority (Jude 6). When God commands us to submit, he means that we should arrange ourselves as God has ordained for the family, the larger society, and the universe. When creatures do not keep their proper place, things fall apart.

In the family, submission is a key concept to ensure proper function. Just like a team with players out of position will experience chaos, so a family with members swapping roles willy-nilly will experience frustration and may generally prove ineffective.

Makers of Home

Contemporary readers often roll their eyes at passages like Proverbs 31 (too idealized), Titus 2:3–5 (too old-fashioned), and other parts of Scripture that seem to describe a brand of womanhood at least as passé as June Cleaver. Our modern sensibilities go to war as we wonder if the biblical writers want women chained to their stoves. We are therefore tempted to dismiss any interpretation of "biblical womanhood" that explicitly connects a woman to her home, but the Bible *does* describe the home as a significant stewardship for wives specifically as they help their husbands cultivate a godly family. So we must reckon with this part of God's game plan.

The Bible consistently exhorts women to be workers at home, which means that they have the sacred responsibility to make their houses—however modest they may be—into real *homes*. Others have written about this extensively and well, but we should consider briefly in this chapter the artfulness of homemaking. A home, after all, is a place where individuals can live and play and worship, where they can welcome friends and practice hospitality toward strangers, where they can reliably find food and clothing and shelter, where they can rest and be safe. A woman who makes a home therefore contributes to the well-being of her family in profound ways.

What about the Sisyphean tasks of housework and meal preparation? A homemaker as described above must necessarily bear the primary responsibility for things that seem mundane and undesirable, like scrubbing toilets and washing dishes—tasks that never seem *done* but that are essential to daily flourishing. Just think about it: if your toilets never get scrubbed, it's hard to ever invite anyone over for tea. For some June Cleaver types, having a clean house can become an obsession, but there is *some* truth to the old adage that cleanliness is next to godliness—at least insofar as some measure of cleanliness ensures an appropriate level of comfort for a home's inhabitants to rest, play, and practice hospitality.

But a woman need not *do* all of these never-ending tasks herself in order to be a Proverbs 31 or Titus 2 woman. Rather, she should wisely *manage* her home in such a way as all its residents learn the glory of homemaking while sharing the tasks that make their house a home. Such workers at home may also do work outside their homes or otherwise earn paychecks, and they should almost certainly serve in some ministry capacity outside their homes. Women should use their spiritual gifts to benefit their families, their churches, and our world. But God's blueprint for family seems to define the home as the foundational sphere in which wives do their God-given "help-meet" work.

On Cultivation

Well before laptops and smartphones, God wanted women active in society while simultaneously cultivating a biblical home environment. We see a poetic portrait of such a woman in Proverbs 31, a Hebrew acrostic that presents an A–Z of biblical womanhood. This industrious lady has full control of her household because she understands the Lord's "game plan" for her family and diligently provides everyone with what they need to execute that plan. She works *from* her home and *for* her home.

The Proverbs 31 woman is breathtakingly productive on behalf of her family. She works relentlessly to supply what her family and society need by importing merchandise, investing in property, crafting products, counseling others, modeling charity, preparing for the future, making her home a haven, and managing her household staff. Her kids dress well, eat well, and generally do well. Her husband is satisfied and trusted, thanks to his excellent wife. She has therefore earned the coveted commendation of God and the grateful thanks of her family.

Some complain that the Proverbs 31 woman lives an impractical life: have you ever heard of a contemporary high-powered business-woman who spends her pre-dawn hours sewing all of her children's clothing? Others have tried to make this passage like a checklist that godly woman should measure themselves against.

So let's get to the heart of this passage by getting to the heart of this woman: she is successful in business, but her identity centers on her fear and love of the Lord, and she expresses it primarily in her roles as wife and mother. She is a model of balanced priorities. After all, the primary activities of this "excellent wife" include helping her husband, providing for her children, and managing her home. Her unusual enterprises outside her home set her apart and certainly keep us from dismissing the chapter as old-fashioned, but her primary work is to help her family flourish. That is the main way in which the excellent woman blesses her world: she cultivates her family, her home, her own giftedness, and her city. The Proverbs 31 woman leads in assists.

On Work Outside the Home

Unfortunately, some women do not find family life fulfilling. Ferrying children to soccer practice and violin recitals feels like drudgery. Cleaning and beautifying the home, overseeing the family's diet, and shopping for supplies seems beneath them. They long for the respect our world gives to financially successful moguls, so they eschew God's game plan and aim their energies at endeavors the larger society admires. There are many circumstances in which a wife and mother might very reasonably work outside the home and glorify God by doing so. But we too often assume these days that a woman's value is primarily, or even only, in whatever work she does apart from the home and family.

We can all thank God for the opportunities contemporary women have to influence and ameliorate society. I know of Christian women devotedly attentive to raising, educating, and nurturing their kids while simultaneously running productive business enterprises. Some women multitask well and can effectively work from their homes in a way that does not at all deprive their husbands of loving wives or their children of attentive mothers. Women should also understand their spiritual gifts and use them in ministry to the church and the world.

Proverbs 31 assumes that women should be educated, equipped, and extolled for the excellence they practice. But at some point, our world began to assume that real excellence happens outside of the home, independent of other family members. We make idols of education and work, and we reduce homemaking to a put-down. Thus, many mothers drop their babies off at day care in order to build careers by choice: they have misplaced their priorities and crave fulfillment outside their family's well-being. This is a disconcerting trend in our world, for when people deliberately choose to neglect God-given priorities for the ephemeral reward of financial success, the results can be devastating.

Of course, many mothers work outside the home by necessity. Single moms, for example, who tackle whatever they must to provide for their children, should be commended. Their double sacrifice of concurrently raising kids and providing financially for them is a testimony of the selflessness that God loves and rewards. But we should regard the difficulty of single parenthood as a sad reality in a fallen world, not the norm.

Many couples will say that families *need* two incomes to survive these days. Dual-income families are so common now that their spending power drives up the cost of living and makes it difficult for single-income families to keep up. We also see more and more young people practicing a mercantile lifestyle as they delay marriage and children, such that it is exceedingly difficult to cut back on spending when they do. We assume that a wife working outside the home is a "necessary evil" if we will afford the "must-have" lifestyle to which we have grown accustomed. But when a wife moves unnecessarily into the workforce, it almost always takes her away from her homeward priorities so that she takes on more than she should bear. The solution, I believe, is not in dividing home duties better but in realigning family priorities.

When a wife embraces her role as helper and does the all-important work of assisting her husband—instead of sharing his same responsibilities, competing with him, or hindering him—she will sense the exhilaration of success. When a mom takes a primary role in equipping her children to grow into who God has made them to be, rather than neglect them to pursue a conflicting agenda, she will reap the reward only a mom can appreciate.

The Worst Fumble in the History of Humanity

As with my hapless high school basketball players, a poor grasp of one's role in the family leads to rivalry where there could be synergy. In Genesis 3, when Satan launches his catastrophic attack on the young family, he does so by undermining the unity God designed for the family. The wife was named her husband's helper before sin ever entered the world, and that is why I have waited until this point in the chapter to discuss the fall, but the family did suffer significant consequences when the Serpent attacked God's good order. Both the man and woman experienced curses from God that became embedded in their fallen nature.

Let's study the instant replay of our first parents' fatal fumble in Genesis 3 and observe the implications for family matters. First, we see the Serpent's opening gambit:

> Now the serpent was more crafty than any other beast of the field that the Lord God had made. He said to the woman, "Did God actually say, 'You shall not eat of any tree in the garden'? . . . You will not surely die. For God knows that when you eat of it your eyes will be opened, and you will be like God, knowing good and evil."
> —Genesis 3:1, 4–5

Remember that God brought Eve to Adam so that he could name her—a sure sign of headship (see 1 Timothy 2:13). But at this crucial moment, the Serpent circumvented Adam's role as head, and the protector/leader failed to intercept the slippery suggestion that God's Word was insufficient.

How did Eve respond? She played the role of spiritual head and led her husband into the temptation:

> When the woman saw that the tree was good for food, and that it was a delight to the eyes, and that the tree was to be desired

to make one wise, she took of its fruit and ate, and she also gave
some to her husband who was with her, and he ate.

—Genesis 3:6

Soon after, God confronted the crestfallen couple. Although Eve
had engaged the Serpent, taken the fruit, violated God's command,
and baited Adam, God addressed Adam first as head of the family
(verse 9). But with a brash new selfishness, Adam shoved Eve out
to face God: "The woman whom you gave to be with me, she gave
me fruit of the tree, and I ate" (verse 12). Adam blamed God as the
incompetent coach who put the woman in the game, and then he
blamed Eve as the weak link in their squad, taking no responsibility
for himself.

The family becomes so vulnerable when we abandon our positions! But we haven't even seen the most chilling implication yet. For
when God cursed the woman, he predicted how Eve's penchant for
usurping headship would play out in the home and society: every
wife would now have the natural tendency to dominate her husband
who would in turn seek to dominate her (see chapter 1 for a longer
discussion of Genesis 3:16). A relationship meant to be a beautiful synergistic dance would now devolve into a horrible tussle of
reciprocity.

Adorning Beauty and Cracking Heads

The curse in Genesis 3 may seem to spell marital doom. How
do husbands and wives ever get along? There is a way! They must
practice a special kind of teamwork that requires tremendous faith
in God's promises. Wives especially must exert faith as they carry
out their assigned assists.

Consider how the apostle Peter said that Christian wives should
follow the leadership of their husbands—even those who may be
blatantly disobedient to God's Word—in an effort to win their husbands over by respectful and pure conduct (1 Peter 3:1–2). Peter
uses Abraham's wife Sarah as an example because she epitomized
otherworldly trust in God to rescue her from her husband's repeated

idiocy. Sarah was apparently physically attractive, but she cultivated an inner beauty that set the bar high for all her spiritual descendants:

> Do not let your adorning be external—the braiding of hair and the putting on of gold jewelry, or the clothing you wear—but let your adorning be the hidden person of the heart with the imperishable beauty of a gentle and quiet spirit, which in God's sight is very precious. For this is how the holy women who hoped in God used to adorn themselves, by submitting to their own husbands, as Sarah obeyed Abraham, calling him lord. And you are her children, if you do good and do not fear anything that is frightening.
> —1 Peter 3:3–6

Abraham, as you will recall from the events recorded in Genesis 12 and Genesis 20 (yep, twice), hatched a scheme to protect himself from powerful men who he feared would kill him to get to his attractive wife. He inflated the half-truth that she was his half-sister into a full-blown lie that she was merely his sister and not his wife. Sarah put her trust in God even when her husband's chicken-hearted decisions put her safety at risk, and that is why Sarah is the submissive supermodel of true inner beauty.

A godly wife treading in Sarah's confident footsteps realizes that her submission to her own husband is actually submission to God, her loving Father. Trusting in God's goodness and power makes it possible for her to follow her husband, even as he may make foolish and disastrous decisions. This does not mean that Christian wives should submit to their husbands into abuse or sin, and a godly pastor would surely have counseled Sarah to appeal to her husband and perhaps even refuse to go along with his plans. If you are married to an inept or ungodly husband, you may need to seek specific counsel about how to live faithfully and wisely in your marriage.

Similarly, husbands tempted to take smug satisfaction in Peter's instruction to wives should read the next verse carefully: "Likewise, husbands, live with your wives in an understanding way, showing honor to the woman as the weaker vessel, since they are heirs with you of the grace of life, so that your prayers may not be hindered" (1 Peter 3:7). A husband has a high calling indeed, and he should never expect his wife to treat him like a leader if he refuses to behave like one.

All this said, we must take 1 Peter 3 simply for what it says and not explain it away too quickly with all of the horrid exceptions and abuses that can occur in our sinful world. We must not take those situations lightly, but we also must not dismiss the principle here: generally speaking, a wife should trust that God is leading her through her husband. More broadly, a godly wife should trust her God completely, and her trust is her singular beauty.

The Bible is replete with examples of bad heads of households. Time would fail us if we tried to name them all, but let's not forget Lamech the first polygamist, Lot who offered his daughters to be raped, Jepthah whose rash vow cost his daughter's life, the antagonistic Nabal who apparently had a death wish for himself and his family, and Manasseh who sacrificed his son to an idol. Only a fool would fail to see why submission is a terrifying prospect for a young bride. But God's promises need to be taken seriously. When husbands fall short, wives have a choice to make: disobey God and dominate, or trust God and follow (within godly bounds) a poor leader.

After all, we must ask whether God can use a loser husband's poor decisions for his glory. Absolutely! Jael is immortalized as an example of a woman who played her role on her family team despite a scary decision that her villainous husband Heber made. We read in Judges 4:17 that Heber had made peace with God's enemy (never a good strategy) and moved away from God's people. This must have caused some consternation for Jael, a godly Jewish lady who loved God and his people, but she moved submissively with her husband, and God used her mightily and memorably. The fugitive enemy general, Sisera, ended up at Jael's tent, so she prepared some milk and cookies and let him nap before finishing the job that General Barak could not do. Judges 5 extols at length Jael's tent-peg assassination. Though a submissive wife, Jael was in no way passive or weak; rather, she was a courageous, godly woman.

Thank God for the MVP

The success of a family unit comes from everyone's willingness to work together as a team, playing their God-given positions to achieve the goal of glorifying God and enjoying the blessings that come from pursuing that goal. Without the wife executing essential "assists," the family flounders like aimless players on the court with no point guard to set up the victories. Thank God for his gracious provision of help and for his infinite wisdom in making the woman undeniably the home team's most valuable player.

Ask Yourself

The wife plays a critical role as helper: she helps the family succeed at giving God glory and enjoying his blessings. Since our world has strived to redefine and denigrate this vital position on the team, it falls to Christian families to example God's design.

1. Wives, in what ways do you fulfill your role of helping your husband lead and provide for the family (e.g., cultivating a home where the gospel is central and God's Word is honored, managing the home in a way that helps your husband earn a living for the family if possible).

2. What are some images that spring to mind when you hear the word *submission*? Is your concept of submission different from God's? If so, imagine that you are explaining the biblical view of submission to a young lady (better yet, have this conversation with a daughter or older girl in your church). What verses do you need to know and understand? Articulating their meaning to someone else will help you internalize what God says is true.

3. If your husband is a spineless jellyfish of a leader, or an ungodly man, or a spiritual slacker who for whatever reason does not lead your family as he should, you can still strive to play your position. In what ways can you still obey God while compensating for your husband's neglect?

4. If the idea of submitting to your husband scares you, address that fear in these three ways:

   a) Read 1 Peter 3:1–6 and ask God to help you play your position.

   b) Find an older godly lady in your church who is playing her position in a gracious and gospel-centered way, and ask her to meet with you occasionally so that you might learn how to apply what she has learned to your life.

   c) If possible, talk to your husband about how you want to help him the way God says you should, and communicate honestly with him about why you find it difficult to do this. You may find that your husband is more open to playing his position when he understands that you want to help him rather than hinder him in that goal.

Note: If you are in an abusive marriage, you should seek counsel and help from your church elders immediately and take whatever action is needed to secure safety for you and your children. When God calls wives to submit to their own husbands, he does not mean that you should suffer abuse.

5

Team Players, Part 1

Little League

Josh Waitzkin was a regular five-year-old kid in a regular family. He feared the dark, struggled to tie his shoes, enjoyed video games, and taunted his little sister. But one day, as he and his mom strolled through Washington Square in New York City en route to the monkey bars, Josh paused to watch some men playing speed chess for cash. He became mesmerized by the nimble manipulation of pieces, the humorous heckling from onlookers, the rhythmic cadence of the chess clock's *click* punctuating the duel. He absorbed, as by osmosis, the patterns for each piece and instinctively grasped the strategy employed to advance the warfare.

Then Josh noticed a seedy-looking elderly man sitting alone at a nearby chessboard and reading a newspaper. Josh dashed away from his mother and planted himself on a chair across from the man, challenging him to a game. The man's face betrayed a combination of incredulity and disgust at the child's presumption. His mother arrived on the scene and apologized for the interruption, explaining that the boy didn't even know how to play chess. But Josh was adamant that he could play; after all, he precociously explained, he had watched two older boys at his school playing earlier that week. Bonnie offered to pay the man if he would humor the boy. He rolled his eyes, grabbed the cash, made an opening move, and promptly returned to his newspaper. After every move Josh made, his opponent deftly nudged pieces around, barely looking up from his reading.[1]

Bonnie would later comment that her scatter-brained little boy's prodigious concentration utterly surprised her. She sensed that if she put her hand between him and the board, his eyes would have burned a hole right through her. But the man suddenly sat bolt upright and began to scold her loudly for hustling him. Apparently, Josh had employed a maneuver that forced the man to put down his paper and concentrate in order to extricate himself from an embarrassing defeat.

Josh Waitzkin lost his first game of chess that day in the park. But shortly afterwards, he became the only person in history to win the national championship title in all six age groups—all before he entered high school. The thing is, most kids are like Josh. They have tremendous potential. They just need the chance to get off the bench and play the game.

Where to Start

Some parents experiment with various training techniques over the years because they have no idea what will work: they just hope that something will stick with their children when they begin to play in the big leagues. Others try to keep their children protected on the bench as long as possible, which means that they essentially throw their kids into the pros at age eighteen with very few skills. Both of these kinds of families operate in survival mode most of the time; the parents may worry over launching their kids too soon or else worry that the kids will never launch, but they just want to make it through this day or this season. The problem is, they're not sure how to do that.

God has not left parents to simply hope that their children will develop into good family players. Rather, he has supplied parents with a terrific user manual: the Bible. The Bible assumes that parents should train their children to actually play the game bit by bit as they grow. Sitting on the bench for nearly two decades won't prepare them to play, but neither will pushing them onto the field early without any training. You must regard every member of the family as an active player, but if you have children, you must diligently train them to participate in family life now and prepare them for whatever the next season holds.

Parents and children need to begin by understanding their respective roles in the family. When this happens, family life will become much more effective and enjoyable. So don't skip over the basic truth that parents are parents and children are children: two distinct categories. God establishes an authority structure in the family that gives parents responsibility for their children, while children have a duty to honor their parents:

> Children, obey your parents in the Lord, for this is right. "Honor your father and mother" (this is the first commandment with a promise), "that it may go well with you and that you may live long in the land." Fathers, do not provoke your children to anger, but bring them up in the discipline and instruction of the Lord.
> —Ephesians 6:1–4)

Note that Paul addresses children directly here, for no one (no matter how young) is immune from biblical responsibility. The fifth commandment that Moses delivered to Israel directly applied to children, and Paul quotes it here to support his instruction. God clearly has great expectations of children and is serious about their responsibility to him.

In this passage, *children* refers to those who live in the same household as their parents. What parent hasn't invoked this basic truism: "As long as you live under my roof, you live by my rules"? We all understand that the one responsible for a household also exercises authority over those under his care. But not all *children* are the same, and *honor* may look different at different stages of maturity. Your family may contain children of various ages and maturity levels, and the range of family members living in your household may vary greatly depending on your culture. Following God's game plan for the family means applying God's wisdom to various stages of family life.

Though God's basic definition for the family is a husband and wife, most of us live in larger families, and most of you reading this book probably have children under the age of eighteen. Because training your children in *honor* looks different at their different stages of maturity, we will discuss childrearing over two chapters. This chapter will consider "little league," or family life with small children in the house, and the next chapter will consider "minor league," or family life with teens.

Obedience School

The American Kennel Club describes obedience trials as opportunities to show that a dog can behave as well in public and even around other dogs as in his own home, and that an obedient dog should appear to enjoy obeying his master. Right. Those of us whose dogs jump on guests, bark at everything, dig up gardens, and flee with their Frisbees into the unknown wilderness look at championship obedience dogs with envy. But the truth is that we are just reaping the harvest of untamed rebellion that we single-handedly sowed through neglect and laziness.

Although the dog that wins an obedience trial gets a blue ribbon and perhaps a sumptuous bone as a deserved reward, the real credit goes to the trainer. No one thinks that the handler was lucky to purchase such an obedient creature from the local pet store. When a puppy comes home, it is a blank slate, waiting to be programmed for either obedience or disobedience. Lazy training leads to untold frustration when a cute puppy becomes a large collection of teeth consuming everything valuable on your patio.

Of course, raising obedient children is a full-time calling much more serious than training dogs. This is why God gives children a simple but profound command to order their hearts: "Children, obey your parents in the Lord, for this is right" (Ephesians 6:1). Obedient children are not a result of winning the genetic lottery; rather, children are commanded to obey because it is not in their nature to do so. To obey "in the Lord" means to respond to one's parents just as one would respond to a command from the Lord himself. Why? Simply because it is right. God's way is the only acceptable way.

Biblical obedience has three parts: 1) immediate obedience without coercion, 2) complete obedience, and 3) heart obedience. Except when a parent's commands would require his children to sin, children should obey quickly and completely with joy. We say it this way in our home: "Obey mommy and daddy the first time, all the way, with a happy heart."

First Time

If a parent must repeat some command at escalating volume, count to three, or threaten punishment in order to get a half-hearted response, he has not merely gotten reluctant obedience but actually a dangerous species of disobedience. In her book *Don't Make Me Count to Three!*, wise mom Ginger Hubbard chides parents for leaning on these kinds of phrases and actions to actually avoid discipline. Indeed, when you count or threaten before expecting obedience, you basically teach your children that sin and rebellion is fine for three seconds; only after that does their behavior become disobedient and therefore warrant punishment.

Imagine this scenario played out in Eden. God tells Adam not to eat the fruit from that tree, and when he does, God says, "Adam, I'm going to count to three, and when I get to three, you need to stop eating the fruit." Adam munches voraciously until the final syllable of "Two-and-a-half," at which point he discards the half-eaten fruit, wipes the dripping evidence from his lips, and breathes a sigh of relief that he narrowly averted the fall of mankind. It would be comical if it were not so convicting.

All the Way

Sometimes children hear "Pick up your toys and go to bed" and then pick up *most* of the toys but start playing with Legos before they finish. That's not partial obedience; it's disobedience. Yes, young children often require reminders, and parents must be wise and give them tasks that they can complete successfully before their immature minds get distracted. But parents should expect their children to remember reasonable commands, and they should teach children to understand that incomplete obedience is simply not an option.

Remember in 1 Samuel 15 when God told King Saul to devote all the Amalekites to destruction, even their livestock? Saul managed to execute *most* of the Amalekites (except King Agag) and *most* of the animals (except a few of the best). Samuel asked ominously, "What is this bleating of sheep I hear in my ears? (v. 14)" and Saul seemed to actually believe that he had obeyed God's command (1 Samuel 15:20). Samuel disagreed, of course, and vehemently declared that Saul had rejected God's Word. In other words, Samuel said partial obedience is disobedience.

With a Happy Heart

Ginger Hubbard explains concisely the importance of the heart in your child's obedience:

> Biblical discipline gets to the heart of the problem. After all, if you can reach the heart, the behavior will take care of itself. . . . There is far more to parenting than getting our children to *act* right. We have to get them to *think* right and to be motivated out of a love of virtue rather than a fear of punishment.[2]

As much as partial obedience offends God, obedience with a begrudging heart is worse. Jesus rebuked the Pharisees for just that attitude since they kept the law externally but also kept sinful attitudes: "This people honors me with their lips, but their heart is far from me" (Matthew 15:8). External obedience with a rebellious attitude and disposition honors neither parents nor God because obedience is ultimately about relationship. Children should obey their parents, but parents should train them in love: ultimately, you want them to *want* to obey from hearts delighted in God.

The Good Life

A young child may take a rather simple perspective on all of this, and that's okay. After all, God speaks their language when he gives them reason to obey their parents' instruction: he promises that they will be blessed and not die. That may seem pretty blunt, but it is exactly what Paul says in Ephesians 6:1–3, basically quoting Exodus 20:12. And the reward for obedience implies dire consequences for disobedience: if honoring your parents secures blessing and long life, then what does dishonor get you? In God's view, a child's obedience to his parents isn't just a good idea. It is serious business.

Left to their own devices, young children will practice folly rather than seek the good life. They will step inadvertently on poisonous jellyfish while blindly imagining that they are pirates running the beach, or they will play with their dolls rather than do their homework. Proverbs 22:15 tells us, "Folly is bound up in the heart of a child, but the rod of discipline drives it far from him." Children do not need to be taught how to lie, shoplift, pull their sister's hair, tease other kids, or avoid their chores. But to allow the dragon of your child's sin nature to go untamed is to ask for forthcoming disaster. Sin and folly come naturally to children, so their parents must diligently instill wisdom in their hearts.

The Bible tells us again and again that discipline is good and loving—indeed that it is unloving *not* to discipline our children (Proverbs 13:24; 23:13–14) and that to discipline our children is a sign of our love for them (see Hebrews 12:9–11). As much as young children protest being disciplined (or pad their pants with tissues), they instinctively recognize that consistent, loving discipline and instruction is a sign of parental involvement and love because it has at heart the child's best interests for a long, good life.

Attention, Not Abandonment

Some parenting philosophies relegate children to a kind of "seen and best not bothered" dungeon. This is a type of abandonment that functionally puts children in a holding pattern of immaturity and ignorance, excluded from meaningful participation in family life. Parents with this mindset fail to engage personally in raising their children. Maybe they view the teaching and training of their children as somebody else's responsibility: schools equip the children for life, Sunday school prepares them for the afterlife, and sports build their character. These parents blame failures and misbehavior on the naughtiness of the child (a mystical condition they caught like a cold) or else the ineffectiveness of teachers.

But young children especially require direct engagement from their parents. Their relentless "Mommy, mommy, mommy" requests are actually an example of this, and it's good; kids need eye contact and full presence. Parental non-involvement actually exasperates children, and it should. Your kids may never tell you this, but they want to know *your* rules. They crave *your* parameters. The kind of loving, attentive involvement that young children need includes copious discipline and instruction.

Active Instruction

Biblically, discipline is much more than punishing wrong behavior. Children need guidance, not freedom. This is why verses like Deuteronomy 6:7 and Ephesians 6:4 exhort parents to get actively involved in bringing up their children. As we discussed in chapter 3, dads carry the ultimate responsibility for this; most kids spend more time with their moms who play invaluable roles in raising children, but Ephesians 6:4 is directed at dads. The command is to "bring them up," not "staff them out," and that involves ongoing "discipline and instruction," not occasional missives of paternal wisdom.

Is there any room in Deuteronomy 6:4–9 for an absentee father or a distant mother? Bringing up one's children is not a one-off formal course of study, like a college degree. It is an ongoing, inductive, life-on-life apprenticeship. Teach your kids how to evangelize, how to respond rightly in a trial, how to tell the truth, how to practice kindness, and how to behave humbly and with integrity. Encourage your kids to forge unlikely friendships and invite their friends to church, and you will find that the parents often come too. But know that children don't learn from dad waxing eloquent so much as they do from dad responding to aggression on the freeway, to disappointment at work, or to bad news in the hospital. Your unscripted life speaks much more loudly than your prepared devotions.

Do not relegate spiritual lessons to a formal Bible hour before bedtime each night. Instead, both parents must conduct such lessons continually in the warp and woof of everyday living. Every billboard of an immodestly dressed woman selling car tires is an opportunity to teach children about God's view of purity "by the way." Every sitcom using lies as a device to drive the humor is a chance to explain the consequences of deception "as you sit in your house." Let your children ask questions, make observations, and give feedback so that you can gauge their spiritual discernment and progressing wisdom.

Friends or Foes

Parents often seem tempted to have a hands-off approach when it comes to selecting a child's friends. It may seem overbearing to meddle in something so personal, but Scripture warns that friends exert tremendous influence over us. The more impressionable your child is, and the more prone to follow rather than lead, the more vulnerable they are to being steered off the rails by unwholesome companions (see 1 Corinthians 15:33). For this reason, Psalm 1:1 is a great text to have young children memorize: "Blessed is the man who walks not in the counsel of the wicked, nor stands in the way of sinners, nor sits in the seat of scoffers."

We find a classic example of a bad decision sprung from the folly of imbecilic friends in 2 Chronicles 10. Rehoboam, son of Solomon and newly crowned king of Israel, receives a request from the citizenry that he ease up on the building projects his father relentlessly pursued. The older government counselors tell him this would be a good way to ingratiate himself to his subjects. Rehoboam then consults his naïve young friends who give him the disastrous contrary advice to increase the workload as a power play. You can guess how well that went. Rehoboam went with his skater buddies' experiment, and it split the kingdom irreparably into a North-versus-South schism.

Not all peer pressure leads to civil war, but much of it will bring ruin to individual lives if left unchecked. Parents have a responsibility before God to help their children forge helpful friendships and guard them from harmful influences.

Who Plays Center?

Children are not the nucleus of the nuclear family. Rather, as we established in chapter 1, a family is formed when a man and a woman leave their parents and form a new, distinct one-flesh unit. The marriage relationship is the core of the family. If mom and dad are unified in their understanding of their responsibility before God and in their parenting strategy, then your children will probably experience happiness and security as a (mostly) natural by-product.

Given our contemporary climate, we must note again that Paul revealed the family hierarchy in no uncertain terms: "Children, *obey* your parents" (Ephesians 6:1), not "Parents, reason with your children and plead with them to do what you want" or "Parents, do everything for your children so that they enjoy innocence and carefree living as long as you can possibly secure it for them" or even "Parents, shield your children from the outside world." We have all seen parents abandon the fundamental truth of Ephesians 6 for a host of other philosophies, so I invite you to reorient your family priorities right now.

Don't Cower

Some parents fear squelching their child's lively personality or confining the child's expressive nature, so this may sound unloving, but biblical wisdom actually says that you must do those things. I do not mean to suggest that you should raise uncreative robots who do not act their age, but children must sometimes be made to curb their inner artist when the time and place requires that they do so. When children sense that they have power over their parents and can do as they wish rather than as they should, the family world begins to fall apart. So we see a mom in the grocery store trying to get her four-year-old son to put down the steak knife by reasoning with him like she's an FBI hostage negotiator ready to accept a list of demands. Will it take cookies, candy, and an extra hour of Playstation to get him to obey? Onlookers may enjoy the entertainment while the poor mom implodes from a combination of embarrassment, concern, and desperation.

Our world has forgotten whom God put in charge of whom. Young children do not need much say in what they wear, what they eat, or what their bedtime is. Why? Because God put their parents in charge. As your children mature in trustworthiness, you should start to introduce reasoning, discussion, and even debate on issues, but only as a way to continue instruction, preparing your children for eventual life outside your home. At no point before your children live independently outside the home should they think of themselves as equal (in role) to their parents. God has placed parents over children in terms of authority—not because they are always right or because they are better human beings but because our God is a God of order. He has not put children at the center of the family, and that is for their good.

Don't Hover

On the opposite side of the spectrum of parental involvement are the parents who micromanage a child's every move. While appropriate to an extent (especially in the early years), this kind of parenting does not produce young adults who are independently dependent on God. The goal of parenting is not to continue guarding your grown children as if they were babies. Parents should want their kids to grow up as responsible, capable adults who can function on their own in the world.

This begins very early when parenting young children. We hold hands when crossing the street only until the child can take the responsibility of watching for cars. We remain with our children during playdates only until they are old enough to stay by themselves at a friend's house. Parents must protect their children from evil but also train even their youngest children to seek and trust their God, especially when they encounter unusual realities in the world. By the time your children spend time outside the home without parental supervision, they should have been trained how to behave, whom to trust, and how to respond in various situations. This can only happen by letting them off the bench and into the game for increasing intervals with decreasing parental involvement.

Don't Shelter

Many parents treat the souls of their children as if they possessed an incurable immune deficiency. Anxious about infecting their young ones with worldly philosophy, they keep them in a sterile environment, never allowing their children to play with other kids or venture outside the home. All their education and entertainment comes directly from their parents. This certainly can preserve your children from worldly influences and may be highly appropriate in the very young years, but at some point, if your children have any hope of surviving independently outside the home, they will need exposure to what is out there.

We must humbly remember the spiritual reality that makes attempts to insulate our children from sin rather futile. The problem of sin that you rightly want to protect your children from does not lie primarily outside your home, no matter how godly it is in practice. The Bible reveals to us that sin is far more insidious than any biological killer. Sin resides in our hearts from birth (Psalm 51:5; 58:3), which means our children come into the world broken; exposing them to worldly vices will not *make* them sinful since they are already that way. Besides, even as you grow in grace, you are sinning against and before your children each and every day. Whatever protective bubble of isolation that you erect, the germs are already inside: you and your children live there.

When you as parents come to grips with the fact that your children are sinners from the womb, you can truly depend on God for their salvation and protection. Instead of taking the whole burden on yourselves, you can enjoy the freedom of knowing that your child's most basic problem is not something you can fix, but a systemic sinfulness that only Jesus the Savior can remove. Of course, this does not mean that you should kick your kids out of the protective bubble early to fend for themselves at young ages. Instead, you should employ a strategy of slow, incremental education of how to deal with sin by relying on the Savior. Realign yourself with gospel reality and accept your profound responsibility to constantly take your child to Jesus in prayer, teaching, and example. You cannot repair your child by yourself, but you can and should take your child to the Savior for rescue.

When you apply the gospel to your parenting, it gives you confidence to get your kids off the bench and in the game so that they can learn how to participate in God's story of redemption rather than just spectate from the sidelines. So help your children give God glory and enjoy his blessings in school, sports teams, clubs, the community, and their future spheres of influence. Children can learn from a very young age the meaning of life and the deep spiritual reasons for why we do anything. You might be as pleasantly surprised by your child's spiritual acuity as Bonnie Waitzkin was at her son's prodigious chess skills.

Ask Yourself

1. Parents, how do you address disobedience in your children? Discuss strengths and weaknesses of the *distinct* ways that you as father and mother discipline the children.

2. Do you reprimand, discipline, and instruct in a biblical way? Do you cultivate obedience in an environment of trust, love, and respect? If not, how can you change the way you address disobedience? (Hint: it may begin with asking your child's forgiveness for your lack of biblical discipline, and making a commitment to pursue consistency in future discipline.) If your children are not yet believers, think of ways that you can bring the gospel to them as you teach and discipline, modeling God's way for them.

3. What are your goals for your children? Do these goals include what God says is important for your child, or are they only worldly goals?

4. Parents, ask your children these questions in an age-appropriate way that they can understand: "Do you think that your attitude and behavior in our home is respectful and obedient? Do you think that you are obeying us in a way that pleases the Lord? Do you see why we discipline you when you disobey us and show us disrespect? Did you know that God commands us to do this? Do you agree that if we love you, we will obey God in this for your long-term benefit?" Plan some times in Bible study that can help your children understand everyone's different roles on the family team.

6

Team Players, Part 2
Minor League

I began the previous chapter with the story of five-year-old Josh Waitzkin who shocked his mother—and, soon, the world—with his tremendous chess skills. I noted that all young children need the opportunity to play just like Josh did, and God has designed the family as the place for them to do that. Kids need caring parents who shape them and maintain safe boundaries in which they can really flourish. God has made young children to be team players, not just spectators or tagalongs.

All this may seem well and good when kids are little and cute, but what about when those tots grow up into tweens and teens? We suddenly typecast our kids as "moody" or "distant" and hunker down for mere survival, figuring that if we can just muddle through, the sass will eventually wear off. Parents often want to be a part of their teens' lives, but they buy into the cultural expectation that "hands off, wallet out, eyes turned" is the only realistic approach to parenting teenagers.

What if you took a different path? What if you stayed present and kept leading your children creatively, watching and listening throughout their teenage years? You might be surprised to find what they can do.

The book Josh Waitzkin's dad wrote about him became a major motion picture, *Searching for Bobby Fischer*, and that movie made Josh an instant celebrity. Yes, even chess has its pop idols. At every tournament, the seventeen-year-old met fanfare and autograph requests, especially from attractive young ladies (chess roadies?), that soon made him dread public appearances. Josh became so distracted that his game suffered, and he eventually quit competitive chess indefinitely.

What would this young man do outside his pre-defined role of chess legend? Many predicted that he would fade into obscurity. But once liberated from limiting expectations, Josh took up a niche Chinese martial art called *tai chi* and excelled beyond all expectations—again. He became the only Westerner to win the world championship gold medal in all three of the sport's disciplines. He has also founded a charity and published books on education, tai chi, and, of course, chess. Not exactly a mediocre life.

Parents of tweens and teens can learn from this story. Our older kids will behave immaturely—they are still growing! But they can and should be taught to behave respectably with exemplary character, just as the apostle Paul advised the youthful pastor at Ephesus: "Let no one despise you for your youth, but set the believers an example in speech, in conduct, in love, in faith, in purity" (1 Timothy 4:12). Notice that Paul did not recommend that Timothy go right on acting the part of youthful pastor because he would grow out of it one day. Neither did he advise Timothy to fend off condescending attitudes toward his ministry by flaunting his job title. Rather, he recommended that Timothy prove his respectability through exemplary behavior (speech, conduct, love) and character (faith, purity). That young man just needed to step into the fullness of his calling.

Young adults should similarly rise to the challenge of exceeding common expectations. The tween and teen years need not be a season of mediocrity or melancholy. Parents should encourage their older children to live well, entrusting them with increasing levels of responsibility and continuing to provide them with instruction and guidance. Your family team can manage the teen years with grace rather than fear.

No More T-ball

T-ball safely exposes tiny tots to the sport of baseball as kids learn to connect their pint-sized bats with stationary targets rather than moving pitches. It's all very cute—for four-year-olds. There are no adult T-ball leagues because everybody knows that T-ball is for kids. Yet some parents indefinitely tee up life's responsibilities for their children instead of intentionally preparing them for the real world.

We achieve maturity—whether physical, intellectual, emotional, or spiritual—through incremental development. So parents must strive to cultivate their children's growth, charting a constant trajectory toward maturity and responsibility by training "their powers of discernment" (Hebrews 5:14). Christian parents prepare their children for a unique kind of independence: they want their children to become independently dependent on Jesus. They therefore bear the primary responsibility of preparing their children to eat solid spiritual food and grow in godliness.

Just like young children, teenagers belong to the family team and must remember that they are still subordinate to their parents. As we pointed out in the previous chapter, that word "children" starting Ephesians 6:1 addresses all dependents in the home—all who have not yet started their own family unit by leaving their mother and father's authority and cleaving to a spouse. A single man of any age who has no job and still lives at home while his parents provide for him has no right to resent their authority over him. As long as children are under the protection and provision of their parents, they need to obey that God-ordained authority structure.

What complicates this is that teenagers feel more responsible, more capable, and more resourceful than they did as younger children. They are in a stage of transition from child to adult. Their parents, meanwhile, may take longer to appreciate this maturity. When teens and their parents see this tension as normal, they can address it together without compromising family unity. Danger strikes when families oversimplify the tension. Teens see the problem as their parents' lack of progressive trust and parents see the problem as their teens' lack of respect for authority. So we must take care not to draw up battle lines but instead to close ranks as a team.

Remember the goal of the family: to glorify God. You must work together toward this end. Parents can help teens do this by getting them outside themselves. This means, according to Paul Tripp in his insightful and practical treatise on parenting teenagers called *Age of Opportunity*, that teens need a glimpse of glory:

> Teenagers desperately need to see the larger story. They need to see their lives as part of something that is bigger and more important than their own happiness. They need a glory to hook into and live for that is bigger than their own glory. They need their story embedded every day in the story of God. This will give them a reason to do what is right. This will give them hope. This will give them strength to endure what God calls them to endure.[1]

If the family will strive for the glory of God—and it must—then teenagers have a unique role to play in that. They're not playing T-ball anymore, but they're still on the family team, and parents have the special challenge of helping them play their changing role well. Begin by recognizing that teenagers bring unique advantages to the family team, like tremendous strength, energy, health, and overall vitality. Teens have an energetic restlessness and healthy discontent that can be harnessed for good and directed into a pursuit of knowledge and social good. They overflow with idealism, which causes them to dream big and tackle intimidating projects with verve. In biblical terminology, young people are blessed with unblinking childlike faith, and "the glory of young men is their strength" (Proverbs 20:29). Think of how simply David responded to intimidation from Goliath.

The Dark Ages

We want our children to maximize their opportunities to worship God and enjoy his gifts while they are still young in body (Ecclesiastes 11:9–12:1). But the teen years are a season of change, of adaption. If you have young adults in your family, you know that helping them spend their time for God's kingdom can prove rather difficult. As your children gain an increasingly broad awareness of themselves and the world (sexuality, politics, economics) as well as new abilities (driving, earning money, influencing their social circles), they grow in power but not necessarily in wisdom. All of this can be confusing and bewildering—both for children and for parents.

Alongside almost every advantage of the teen years, we see a new set of dangers. Temptation is common to every stage of life—no age group is immune from Satan's lure—but the teenage years are a season in life when certain temptations suddenly escalate, and even the most spiritually mature teens often find themselves struggling. These intense temptations can bring dark times, which is why Paul warned the relatively young Timothy rather strongly to "flee youthful passions and pursue righteousness, faith, love, and peace, along with those who call on the Lord from a pure heart" (2 Timothy 2:22). Let's consider some of these "passions" or desires that seem endemic to youth.

Sexual Vulnerability

When hormones start raging, new temptations assault young people, so they need to have been prepared and fortified to practice self-control over lust. If you watch television sitcoms, romantic movies, or eavesdrop on locker-room braggadocio at school, it may seem that all kinds of sexual activity before marriage is normal these days. Are Christians just being old-fashioned or prudish to insist on chastity?

No, even Paul exhorted the Thessalonians to wage war on their society's norm of premarital sex (1 Thessalonians 4:3–5). The culture may change, but God's standards remain the same. Even some Christian circles may condone much sexual indulgence, but we must remember how Jesus turns us inward to the heart, for "everyone who looks at a woman with lustful intent has already committed adultery with her in his heart" (Matthew 5:28). This is why Joshua Harris, in his helpful book *Not Even a Hint*, says that God's standard remains the same regardless of our cultural context or age:

It's not just the sins of adultery and sex outside of marriage God wants us to be freed from; he wants us to eliminate any kind of impurity in our thoughts and actions. He wants us to dig down into our hearts and uproot sexual greediness, which is always seeking a new sensual thrill.[2]

Teens want to know *why* this is God's standard for his people, and that's a fair question, especially when it seems like everything inside them and everyone outside them calls that standard crazy. Harris answers this beautifully: "It's not because God is heavy-handed, or strict for the sake of strictness. It's because he loves us—and because we are his." The bottom line is that when God calls teens to practice self-control during their most lustful and chaotic and confusing years, it's because he loves them.

Young people are particularly vulnerable to lust because of natural curiosity, fueled by good hormones. In a world that mocks self-control and encourages experimentation, parents must remind their teens often and compassionately about what God wants for them. This means talking frankly with them about the benefits of chastity and the bitterness of immorality. You might use Proverbs 7 as a conversation starter, reading together how this wise father vividly portrays the nature and perils of seduction. He describes a temptress speaking every love language to capture a naïve young man, trapping him in a fatal attraction.

Some parents resign themselves to the assumption that sexual experimentation is a natural part of growing up, but God is clear that sex outside the safety of the marriage covenant is not natural. In fact, he says that it is destructive. Paul countered the "it's only natural" argument popular in Corinth with this sobering warning: "The body is not meant for sexual immorality, but for the Lord, and the Lord for the body" (1 Corinthians 6:13). Sexuality is a good gift from God, but we must learn self-control lest our lusts take over and we find ourselves powerless to stop when things go awry. Only grace applied to the heart can help us see God's design for us as good and then help us pursue it with zeal and joy.

Pride

Mohammed Ali was a boxing legend in his own time. Unfortunately, he was also a legend in his own mind. Some called it simple self-confidence, but it's hard to define his comments ("When you are as great as I am, it's hard to be humble," and "I'm not the greatest; I'm the double greatest") as anything less than downright boastful. Ali made the mistake of believing that physical strength and ability make us great. But this is a common error, especially among young people.

The law of Moses actually legislated a practice meant to instill a cultural axiom about humility and honoring the wisdom of the aged. More than common courtesy, it was national law: young adults had to literally stand in the presence of their elders (Leviticus 19:32). Later, Paul instructed Timothy to pastor older men and women with particular care, regarding their age with honor even as he exhorted them in the truth (1 Timothy 5:1–2). If we still practiced such signs of respect in the West, it might be easier for youth to remember the biblical truism that life experience brings wisdom that one cannot learn from a smartphone or the Internet.

Youthful pride can fuel a rather unbecoming attitude. A quick roll of the eyes says, "We have all of the latest gadgets, lingo, fashion, and brands. What else could we need?" The Bible has a name for people who are not humble enough to embrace guidance from others: "'Scoffer' is the name of the arrogant, haughty man who acts with arrogant pride" (Proverbs 21:24) and "A wise son hears his father's instruction, but a scoffer does not listen to rebuke" (Proverbs 13:1). Sound like anyone you know?

Young people have a natural tendency to think of themselves as indestructible know-it-alls. Uncorrected, they will spurn instruction and throw themselves into unwise situations. But God's grace teaches us to number our days rightly, listen respectfully to the wise, and serve others sacrificially. Parents have a solemn duty to train their children—including their teenagers—to practice such humility of heart and mind.

Laziness

Debilitating sloth is by no means a malady limited to youth, but it seems particularly common among those nestled in the warm cocoon of parental overprotection. When parents fail to teach their children to take responsibility, cultivate a good work ethic, and operate diligently in the world, the result is often a tragically inert blob of wasted potential known in the Proverbs as the sluggard. Know anyone who is chronically disorganized, allergic to initiative (20:4), and always starting projects but never finishing them (24:27; 18:9)? The sluggard has also become skilled at several activities you wouldn't want to write home about: he has mastered creative excuses (22:13), naps (26:14), and know-it-all attitudes (26:16).

The family team must work together to help everyone, but especially teenagers, use their time wisely. We must pay special attention to electronic devices as most of us these days carry strong temptation to sloth in our hip pockets. The contemporary entertainment industry specifically targets young people with all manner of digital distraction and electronic escapism: social media networking alone constantly draws us from real relationships and responsibilities to glassy-eyed virtual ones. Teach your children to use technology well so that it operates as their productive servant rather than draining taskmaster. Then you can help them cultivate a biblical work ethic. Control over gadgets comes only from control over self.

Shining Light into the Darkness

Don't be afraid to get specific with your teenagers about temptations that they will face. They may hear frank talk from their friends and see provocative images that celebrate sexual immorality, pride, and laziness, so parents must get bold and direct. Righteous behavior alone is not the goal; godly parents ultimately want their teens' hearts to glorify God, and godly sexuality is an outworking of that. Therefore, brace yourself to ask tough questions as you help your teens learn self-control in the areas of sexuality, self-regard, and diligence.

Young adults will face frequent temptation during this season of their lives and beyond, so one awkward conversation will not be the spiritual cold shower that drives away their lust or the spiritual hammer that kills their pride or the spiritual spur that gets them off the couch. If the onslaught of temptation seems unrelenting, parents need to exhort their children just as often to fight by God's grace. Speak with them honestly, and speak with them frequently.

Talk with your teens about God's purposes in making bodies like he did, and encourage them to adopt healthy disciplines for their bodies as well as healthy relationships with other people. This means helping your children exercise, eat well, and serve others in regular ministry. It means providing accountability for how they text, use social media, and otherwise spend their "screen time." And it means initiating honest conversation. Do not feed your children lies—especially about sex—or even threats that you hope will curb recklessness and scare them into good behavior. That approach is jejune and irresponsible. Instead, discuss God's glorious purposes for your teens as whole persons while educating them about the enslaving consequences of sexual immorality, pride, and laziness.

Let's be honest: this will probably feel awkward for teens and parents alike. But the best place for instruction about spiritual and physical warfare is in the home. Be bold and understanding as you acknowledge the specific temptations that your particular teen might face. Embrace the awkwardness and craft a game plan to address these topics with confidence and avoid vague, impromptu, foot-shuffling monologue. Engage your child's heart for the glory of God.

The Rite Stuff

Mother birds have a natural instinct to nudge their chicks out of the nest so that they develop their wings before they get too fat and heavy to do so. Unfortunately, some human parents resist this kind of training with their own offspring. Instead, we have invented a graded process for maturity with no real beginning and no defined ending: we call the teenage phase *adolescence* now, which means we can treat young adults like children in many areas while chiding them for their irresponsibility. Adolescence bears little resemblance to the kind of training and maturation we see mandated and expected in the Bible.

Sociologists have begun studying another new phenomenon among young adults—especially men—who continue to live with their parents well into their twenties or thirties. Partly owing to the difficulty some have in finding self-supporting jobs, we now see single thirty-somethings living rent free with their parents, languishing in the responsibility-light limbo of perpetual study and/or play. Parents provide laundry, meals, and transport while occasional barista work pays for entertainment. These grown children may think they are in heaven, but they suffer from Peter Pan syndrome, apparently unable to grow up as they live in a bizarre state of semi-responsibility.

Maybe we need to recapture the idea of a rite of passage.

I have a friend whose hunter dad taught him that children are too young to hunt; guns are lethal, animals are unpredictable, and the dangerous African bush is no place for youngsters. His dad would leave him behind with mom during hunts, returning later with riveting tales of his manly bravado. But as my friend approached puberty, his dad announced that it was time he became a man. He taught his son how to shoot, track, and gut an animal. He also allowed his son to accompany the men on their hunts.

One day, his dad said he was ready. He gave him a rifle and told him to go shoot a deer, gut it, and take a bite of its raw liver. This was their family's rite of passage from boyhood to manhood. Pretty gross, if you ask me; it's enough to convert anyone to vegetarianism. But after that day, my friend walked with a swagger and approached life with a newfound seriousness. His parents entrusted him with greater responsibility, and he, in turn, sensed the need to not disappoint them. Of course, at school we still treated him like the pipsqueak he was, hunter or not. But I have to admit there was a twinge of envy in me. Not that I craved raw liver, but I envied that defining moment that swept away my friend's puerile insecurities and ushered him into adulthood.

Jewish culture has a more codified rite of passage known as the bar mitzvah for boys or bat mitzvah for girls, and it occurs around the age of thirteen. Children are considered to have come of age when they take the vows of the covenant for themselves, and they are then expected to behave as those accountable to the law. Indeed, true maturity reflects behavior, not just age: "Even a child makes himself known by his acts, by whether his conduct is pure and upright" (Proverbs 20:11). This verse assumes that children are given *opportunity* to perform "pure and upright" acts—which means they are being trained in responsibility.

Children entrusted with very little will have little with which to impress, but children given increasing opportunity to excel can indeed become excellent. Consider how Israelite youngsters behaved as responsible adults when circumstances required them to do so:

- David was a youth when he defied the giant that caused King Saul and the entire Israelite corps to quiver in their sandals.
- Josiah, who took the throne at age eight, was maybe fifteen when he single-handedly instituted the most widespread and revolutionary reform Israel had seen since Moses had brought the law generations before.
- Daniel and his teenage friends repeatedly and fearlessly stood up to their Babylonian captors.
- Mary's Magnificat demonstrated an outstanding grasp of theology and piety at age thirteen or fourteen, and she followed that paean of praise with a treacherous and uncomfortable journey to submit to her government's paperwork requirements.

These young people did not hide behind the inexperience or vulnerability of their age. They did not perpetually suckle on their parents' good provision but took advantage of their training and held increasing responsibility for themselves: they were expected to conduct themselves with maturity, and they did so. How can we train our contemporary teenagers for the same kind of excellence?

Don't Provoke

Young children who panted for playful freedom under overprotective parents are likely to lash out in flagrant disrespect as teens, but children who experience regular and age-appropriate training from their parents have a good foundation of open and respectful communication on which to build as they grow into teenagers. Yearning for independence, teens will feel out their boundaries, but they can and should do this with ongoing parental instruction and shaping that equips them for adulthood. Because this discipline and instruction process will look markedly different in different societies and circumstances, parents must keep the basic goal in mind: play the game of life in whatever position God has set for them and not just warm the bench as spectators.

The shifting boundaries of maturity will naturally produce some conflict in families, but this conflict need not be constant. Parents of teens will need to drink deeply and often from the fountain of grace to continue in this God-given responsibility with compassion and kindness, not needling: "Fathers, do not provoke your children to anger, but bring them up in the discipline and instruction of the Lord" (Ephesians 6:4). Think about how teens get discouraged when you treat them "like children"—requiring too early a curfew, for example. As children mature, their privileges should safely extend to match their maturity; when overprotective parents neglect to give increasing responsibility, growing children will become frustrated and may even rebel.

Instead of this "provoking" parenting style, Paul offers an alternative: "bring them up in the discipline and instruction of the Lord." This means actively responding to poor behavior and attitudes (correcting, punishing, and implementing consequences) while actively teaching what honors the Lord. Parenting is not just an electric fence that shocks kids with consequence when they transgress boundaries, and it certainly does not consist of repeated reprimands for breeches of trust. Rather, parenting requires proactive teaching of what is good, right, and acceptable. This takes forethought, wisdom, and effort from parents, but it results in children increasingly equipped for responsibility.

Ready, Set, Launch

Let's consider the second clause in Ephesians 6:4 as it relates to teenagers. The word "discipline" here is the Greek word *paideia*, which refers primarily to shaping the *behavior* of the child. The concept involves providing guidance, limits, structure, and punishment for disobedience. But discipline must be accompanied by its twin *instruction*, which is the Greek word *nouthesia*. This term refers to setting one's thinking straight. So it is the Christian parent's task to mold not only the child's behavior according to what is acceptable and productive but also the child's understanding, attitudes, and knowledge of God according to God's Word.

Legendary batsman Babe Ruth was famous for his record-setting home run statistics, but equally prodigious was his strikeout rate. He swung hard at *everything*, and when he missed, he missed big, but when he connected, he thrilled a generation. Effective parenting similarly gives teenagers a chance to strike out, partly because such parenting wants to produce teenagers who require less and less parental involvement. Some parents are paralyzed by the prospect of their children not walking with God, so they try to insulate their children and keep them from making mistakes. This may work as long as the children remain at home, but they will eventually need to leave the safety of the T-ball field.

Prepare your teens (and yourself) for their adulthood through incremental exposure to real challenges. This will help your children mature, especially if they are believers. Christians who grow up completely isolated from other beliefs, practices, and worldviews will never hone their skills to defend the faith (a Christian duty according to 1 Peter 3:15). Of course, children should be protected from attacks on their faith until it has been firmly established in their hearts and lives, but there comes a time when adolescents need to be exposed to opposing viewpoints, if under close supervision by their parents or other wise counselors. Some parents prolong insulation to the point of isolation and therefore do a disservice to their children. These parents could actually be guilty of neglecting the command to train their children.

During the shameful decades of apartheid, South Africa was banned from international athletics in the hope that such pressure would force the government to allow free and fair democratic elections. When the strategy finally worked, South Africa was again permitted to participate in the Olympic Games, but South African athletes had stagnated after so many years of isolation from international competition. The country's best fencers finished last in the 1992 Olympics because we had for a generation only fenced one another. Similarly, parents who shield their older children from challenges will probably find their children ill equipped for the real world.

But parents who study their children and give them age-appropriate opportunities to fail along with a safe place to retreat and learn will find their children courageous and capable in the world. This is what happened to South Africa's best fencers, who took every chance they could after the international doors reopened to fence superior opponents from other countries. The whole team began to improve as a result. Your family team can also benefit when your teens experience challenges and even failure.

Where Do They Learn This Stuff?

The character of your children is forged primarily at home as they play their parts in the family team, and the teenage years are crucial. This season is most certainly an "age of opportunity." Actively continue to shape your teens' thoughts and behavior as they prepare to leave home. You will then take on a different role as you watch how they carry themselves into the world.

That said, you must remember that God does not keep score based on outcomes. As Stuart Scott and Martha Peace wrote in their excellent book *The Faithful Parent*, "The goal of the Christian parent is to be faithful to God's Word by his grace and for his glory. You see, in Christ we have the great hope that we can be faithful whether our children are faithful or not."[3] The family is a team. It stands together and it falls together. By God's grace, we share the effort and the rewards. But as a parent, I find great relief in the fact that God calls me to live faithfully according to his design while leaving the scorekeeping up to him.

Ask Yourself

God has a unique position for young adults to play. The home team can benefit greatly if mom and dad train their children to act responsibly and then give them opportunities to do that.

1. Parents, in what ways do you frustrate your young adult children (e.g., treat them as if they are still tiny tots, give them too much freedom and then punish them for not coping with that freedom, fail to make your expectations clear)?

2. Ask your teen if some part of your parenting style, rules, or reasons frustrate them. Do not respond immediately, but pray about what you hear. If you cannot justify biblically why you do what you do, consider changing your methods to show your teen respect and love. If you can justify your parenting decisions biblically, then think about how you can shepherd your child's heart to understand why you do what you do.

3. In what ways can you help your young adult children prepare for the responsibility of adulthood? Make a specific plan to do this better.

4. When you express disappointment in your teen's behavior or attitudes, do you also explain the larger story of what part she plays in the family so that her motivation is based on pleasing God, not just jumping through parental hoops?

5. Do you know your teen's friends? Are you aware of what he watches, reads, and listens to, and how much time he spends doing those things? How about his social media accounts? What can you do to be more involved (without becoming stifling) and help him make wise decisions about what he exposes his heart to?

7

Team Solo

Singleness and the Family of God

As a younger, more limber version of myself, I fenced competitively at a national level for six years. Fencing is a thrilling and intense sport, but it lacks the camaraderie of most other sports: even in team events, fencers face each bout individually, just you and your masked adversary. Once the duel begins, no gallant musketeers can help you on that lonely piste (the 8-by-1.5-meter strip of metal on which fencers face each other).

My experience as a fencer made me watch with empathy a particularly devastating debacle during the 2012 Summer Olympic Games in London. The ladies épée semifinal match was as tense as any I had ever witnessed. Germany's Britta Heidemann and South Korea's Shin A-Lam finished in regular time at a score of 5–5, pushing the bout into a dramatic one-minute sudden-death overtime. Whoever scored the next touch would make the final and have a shot at Olympic gold. But because Shin had a priority advantage, she merely had to prevent Heidemann from scoring and she would get the win.

In the final second of that long minute, Heidemann and Shin both scored simultaneously. The clock stopped, but because the tie was not yet broken, the bout restarted, and they both scored simultaneously again. The clock had counted down to 0:00 but had not buzzed yet, meaning there was technically still a fraction of a second left. Video review later showed that only about two 100ths of a second remained. But the electronic clock's display could not accommodate such accurate time keeping, so the time keeper and presiding referee decided to reset the clock to a full second, the lowest time the technology could manage. In that eternal second, Heidemann took three stabs at her desperately flailing target, and precisely as the buzzer sounded, the German scored a single touch, which secured her victory.

Pandemonium instantly erupted among the South Korean coach, team, and supporters. Everyone knew this inexcusable technical glitch was to blame for the result. Shin's coaches passionately and persistently appealed the decision all the way to the top authorities. Meanwhile, in a sinister twist of fate, Shin had to remain on the piste since, according to Olympic rules, the fencer challenging the result must stay or forfeit the appeal. So the distraught and exhausted young lady sat on the lonely metal strip weeping uncontrollably as she awaited a verdict. This fiasco dragged on *for seventy minutes.*

Even fencers sometimes find fencing difficult to watch. It's basically watching blurry metal for a few busy seconds at a time, followed by a buzz and a light indicating whom to cheer for. You usually don't have to wait long. So after an hour without any blinking lights at that semi-final match, the popcorn-munching crowd began to get antsy and started to slow-clap in protest of the protest. Meanwhile, Shin had to just sit in front of them as if she was the problem.

Can you feel her loneliness in that moment? I choked up watching her agony. But behind the scenes, many busied themselves on Shin's behalf. Her teammates took the situation personally, and her coach vociferously objected and passionately gesticulated to the referee as he undertook the appeal. As abandoned as Shin must have felt on the piste, she was not really alone. She just seemed alone.

Sometimes in the church, single people feel just like Shin A-Lam during that appeal: alone, stuck, and left out. Married people can treat singleness as if it were a disease to be cured or else a distasteful, immature stage one should grow out of. Well-meaning matchmakers offer unsolicited assistance to fix the "problem," which usually involves a blind date or some such sitcom solution. Instead, the church should play like a team, learning God's playbook as it relates to nuclear family but also as it relates to his heavenly family. We need to come alongside one another, just as Shin A-Lam's team rallied with and for her during her courageous but difficult hour on the piste.

Singles in God's Family

In her sardonically titled book *Why Isn't a Pretty Girl Like You Married? . . . and Other Useful Comments*, Nancy Wilson tells the story of a church dinner that she and her family attended where the "singles" were asked to stand and introduce themselves. Because her daughter was among the unmarried people in the room, Wilson began thinking differently about the term *singles* as it relates to people in the church:

> Our individualistic culture wants to label unmarried people as *singles*, but in the covenant community of God, there are no *singles*. God calls us family: brothers and sisters, mothers and fathers in Christ. We are each to be wonderfully connected to the other as part of a church community, where each person is needed and attached to others in her own family as well as to the broader church family.[1]

I agree with this premise and would even go as far as to say "singles groups" in churches are misnomers. But I still want to address those who are not married in this book because they play a unique role within their own nuclear families and in the larger church family. God creates us as individuals, yet he makes all believers complete in Christ by adopting us into an interconnected family of his children, the church, which is called "the household of God" (1 Timothy 3:15). Every member of an earthly family has an important role to play on the "home team," and every Christian has an important role to play in the local church family as well (see 1 Corinthians 12).

Paul addresses the unmarried in some depth in 1 Corinthians 7:25–33, presenting a clear biblical view on singleness: the state of being unmarried involves various challenges but also has various spiritual advantages and should therefore be considered a blessing rather than a curse. The ESV translates the Greek word for "virgins" as "betrothed" here, to indicate that Paul probably means youth at home and others who have never been married, as opposed to widows or divorcées, but the principle may apply to others as well. When Paul says he has "no command from the Lord" (verse 25), he means that Jesus never issued a command that such persons *must* be married or *must* stay single. Rather, that is a personal choice, or a Christian liberty. But Paul does offer his own opinion, which he reminds his readers is "trustworthy" (not Paul's own interpretation but doctrine inspired by the Holy Spirit, as per 2 Peter 1:20–21 and 2 Timothy 3:16). Simply put, Paul does not forbid marriage but says singleness should be honored.

Some misinterpret this passage when they aver that people who want to be really holy should remain unmarried and take vows of perpetual celibacy. Paul specifically refutes this teaching in verse 28 and elsewhere calls teaching that forbids marriage a demonic doctrine (see 1 Timothy 4:1–3). Marriage is entirely up to the individual believer's conscience, not a matter of choosing a more or less holy path. This is a lesson married people need to learn. Married folk in churches often put great pressure on single people to get married. While those who know the blessings of marriage usually mean well, merely wanting to share their boon with others, this may inadvertently send the message that singleness is an inferior status. The Bible says the opposite.

Once married, we often forget that we were single once, and that unmarried people are not missing out on everything good. Not necessarily, anyway. It's just a different season, and we should quit acting like single people should do everything possible to escape their singleness. One book on dating explains that some unmarried people do feel incomplete, which can make them rather sensitive to pressure from friends who seem to act like they are helpless to find a spouse.[2] So it behooves married people especially to put aside the memories of their misspent singleness and diligently avoid rubbing salt in the wounds of their single friends, focusing instead on counseling the unmarried to capture their advantageous state for the goal of glorifying God.

Remember the Various Reasons for Singleness

This may seem obvious to you, but in case it isn't, let's remember that not all single people are unmarried for the same reason. Jesus noted some possibilities in Matthew 19:11–12 as he taught on marriage and divorce. He discussed eunuchs—men who were unable to procreate and who could therefore access certain careers that other men could not have, like personally guarding females in the royal harem. Jesus mentions that some men were born physically incapable of procreation while others were castrated against their wills (slaves were sometimes treated this way to "protect" females in the household). Still others chose never to marry (it is unclear whether these were always physically eunuchs). The point made here is that most people want to get married, but some cannot, and others choose not to marry at all. Jesus acknowledges that all of these can be good ways to live.

Involuntary Singleness

Let's first consider those single people who wish they weren't so single. Married people can be rather insensitive to the fact that the very friend they jokingly chide for not being married may desperately want a mate but be unable to find a suitable one. Nancy Wilson colorfully explains that newly married women can become patronizing to unmarried women in the church, such that "Her old friends, rather than wishing her well, would prefer to kick her in the ankle."[3] Meanwhile, men who have been blessed enough to find excellent wives sometimes forget that doing so is as special and uncommon as finding a rare jewel (Proverbs 31:10).

A suitable spouse is not a matter of ordering a product customized to specifications. Rather, a spouse is a gift from God (Proverbs 18:22; 19:14). Until God made a suitable companion for Adam and presented her to him as a gift, Adam was powerless to fill that gap in his life (Genesis 2:18). Married people must work at remembering these truths for the sake of their own marriage but also for their unmarried friends and family. Everyone connected to your team needs your sensitive encouragement. Don't take jokes about singleness lightly. Rather, edify your unmarried friends or offer sound practical advice, but never belittle them. Doing so picks a fight with God's sovereign will that He has placed in their lives. He is the one who gives a husband or a wife, and always at the right time—if at all.

Temporary Voluntary Singleness

During some seasons in a person's life, a romantic relationship may be undesirable or unwise. For example, people might postpone thoughts of marriage while they focus on pursuits that would be impractical or inappropriate while married. Some courses of study, like medicine, demand so much time and energy that it may be prudent to get past the worst of it before marrying, so as not to subject a family to the absentee student-worker lifestyle. Take care, though. It is not necessarily sinful or foolish to delay marriage for these reasons, but doing so indefinitely for the sake of blazing one's career path is dangerous, if only because the mindset can prove difficult to change when it comes time for family.

Take as another example those recovering from the emotional pain of a failed romantic relationship: these men and women need time to think and heal, so they should probably not jump quickly into another relationship (Proverbs 13:12). Every coach understands the need for injured players to recover properly; returning to the game prematurely may cause lasting damage. But the pain of broken relationships can take longer to heal than physical maladies (Proverbs 18:14). Family and friends must work as a team to support a single person's need to regroup and recover, avoiding that glib "plenty of fish in the sea" consolation as well as trite and premature pep talks about getting "back in the saddle."

Finally, some young people may receive counsel from their spiritual leaders to avoid romantic relationships, at least for a time. Perhaps they need to mature, overcome an addiction, or pursue some profitable spiritual project. Others, quipping that they're "not getting any younger" or that their proverbial biological clocks are ticking, would certainly add unnecessary pressure in such a situation. Limit your counsel to serious conversations that start with questions to help you understand what words (if any) would be truly wise to say.

Permanent Voluntary Singleness

As difficult as it may be for married readers to imagine, some people actually prefer not to be married. Gasp! And, get this . . . that decision is just fine with God. Jesus did say that it was better not to marry if possible, and he called that state of contentedness a gift from God (Matthew 19:11). But why would God give a gift of singleness to anyone? Paul answers that question when he recognizes the advantages of singleness in 1 Corinthians 7, so we'll consider his words carefully in the next section of this chapter.

Recognize the Various Advantages of Singleness

Some exemplary Christian men and women chose to remain single: Francis of Assisi, Thomas Aquinas, Thomas à Kempis, David Brainerd, Charles Simeon, Dietrich Bonhoeffer, Amy Carmichael, and John Stott, to name a few. And let's not forget that Jesus himself was a perfectly complete and contented individual who never married. Jesus acknowledged that marriage wasn't for everyone (Matthew 19:11), and Paul said that the marital status of a believer (whether married or single) is a "gift from God" (1 Corinthians 7:7).

As a young man who unequivocally desired marriage, I confess that I sometimes facetiously referred to the gift of singleness as "the dreaded gift." There were times before I met my wife when I wanted to ask God if he required a receipt to exchange my singleness for another gift that fit me better. I could not understand why God had me waiting for marriage. But the Spirit used his Word to change my mind, and I began to realize the blessings of singleness.

Fewer Family Responsibilities

You take on responsibility when you must concern yourself with someone else's well-being. Married people do not have their own lives;

they are inextricably enmeshed with their spouses. And if children join the family, the quantity and quality of responsibility increases exponentially. This is good, but it's rough. Many singles are free of such difficulties. Of course, most unmarried people do have some family responsibilities, such as aging parents (1 Timothy 5:8, 16). But they usually share such obligations with siblings and other support structures. Marriage is different because it assigns you a person for whom you have direct responsibility.

> I think that in view of the present distress it is good for a person to remain as he is. Are you bound to a wife? Do not seek to be free. Are you free from a wife? Do not seek a wife. . . . I want you to be free from anxieties. The unmarried man is anxious about the things of the Lord, how to please the Lord.
>
> —1 Corinthians 7:26–27, 32

One difference between talented athletes who make it big and equally gifted individuals who don't is the ability to perform under pressure. Some people thrive when more is at stake, but other people crash. That's my excuse for never being good at basketball: I could throw an endless stream of perfect "swooshes" from the free-throw line in my parents' driveway, but as soon as I had an audience, I lost it. So too, we generally find danger less intimidating when we don't have others depending on us. When Paul says singleness is better in "the present distress," he probably means that unmarried people could handle persecution more easily than married people because no one else depends upon them. Because they have responsibility for more than just themselves—because more than their own lives are at stake—married people might more strongly feel the temptation to recant.

Christians through the ages have suffered distress, as they still do today in many places in the world, and Paul knew that some married Corinthians thought that changing their marital status would somehow solve the tension they felt under persecution. He quickly tells them, then, that married people bailing on their spouses will not help anything. At the same time, he advises unmarried people to remain single. Christians can muster amazing courage in seasons of persecution, energy in moments of fatigue, and sacrifice in time of need, but no one should neglect spouse or endanger children. The responsibility to protect and provide for a family changes the game entirely. But single people risk only their own necks when they step into danger, and that can be quite liberating.

I was in Egypt shortly after the January 2011 revolution that overthrew Hosni Mubarak as president. With no police force, no courts in session, and no local government, pockets of extremists stirred up a volatile mob mentality against Christians, bulldozing churches and burning believers' houses. The "present distress," to use Paul's phrase, was palpable and unnerving. I met many indigenous Christian families who feared for their lives and would have fled to safety in a stable country if they had the opportunity to do so.

But I also met several foreign missionaries, both men and women, who hunkered down to minister to trapped believers. Sending boards were wisely evacuating missionary families until the violence subsided, but some waived their right to be evacuated, opting to remain and face the gnashing teeth of danger. These intrepid servants brimmed with excitement at the prospect of their Lord using them amid political mayhem. And do you know what these brave stalwarts all had in common? They were unmarried. Unencumbered by the weight of responsibility for spouse and children, they could fearlessly fulfill their calling.

Undivided Devotion to the Lord

In 1887, when China Inland Missions deployed an unprecedented 100 missionaries to extend the Protestant outreach effort in Asia, 50 of the qualified candidates were unmarried women! These ladies understood the stewardship of singleness that Paul described; fewer earthly responsibilities naturally means freedom to do the Lord's work without distraction. All mature believers will want to involve themselves deeply in God's work on earth, and God grants us opportunities in different measure as we move through various life stages.

Being single is a time of unparalleled potential to invest time, energy, and finances in kingdom work.

My heart is warmed when I hear of a person attending two Bible studies a week, teaching a group of youth, playing in the worship band, helping widows maintain their homes, and frequently travelling on short-term missions trips. Pastors love to put this type of tireless servant to work in the church! But very few married people can do all of this without neglecting their families, so I would (perhaps reluctantly!) counsel married volunteers to reconsider their priorities. Marriage and children are good and godly distractions, and Paul does not condemn spouses who are "anxious about worldly things" (1 Corinthians 7:33, 34). Instead, he simply states an axiomatic reality: spouses who do not take care of each other are neglecting their God-given priorities, but unmarried people are free to care about other things.

> I want you to be free from anxieties. The unmarried man is anxious about the things of the Lord, how to please the Lord. But the married man is anxious about worldly things, how to please his wife, and his interests are divided. And the unmarried or betrothed woman is anxious about the things of the Lord, how to be holy in body and spirit. But the married woman is anxious about worldly things, how to please her husband. I say this for your own benefit, not to lay any restraint upon you, but to promote good order and to secure your undivided devotion to the Lord.
>
> —1 Corinthians 7:32–35

No one is born married. We all have seasons free from the blessings of matrimonial distraction, and those seasons of unmarried liberty are times to invest your time, energy, money, relationships, and gifts in kingdom work. Though some singles may have children to raise and older singles especially may have their own aging bodies to consider, unmarried people should take whatever opportunities they can to serve the local church. This can mean mundane tasks like helping clean the church during the day (how's that for retirement?)

or running neighborhood ministry programs. And it can include many exciting opportunities in missions and other volunteer work that require mobilization and instability—factors single people can manage far better than their married friends.

Unfortunately these days, freedom from responsibility and distraction usually translates into time and money spent more on self than on others. Compare that to pastor John Wesley's practice of earning as much as he could in order to give all he could. As a bachelor most of his life, Wesley calculated that to live comfortably, his monthly expenses amounted to 28 pounds. In 1731, he earned 30 pounds per month as a lecturer at Oxford University, but as his salary increased to 60, then 90, and eventually 120 pounds a month, Wesley continued to live off of precisely 28 pounds, giving the rest to charity and the work of the gospel ministry. Imagine what good can be done for the kingdom of God when unmarried people focus on ministry rather than themselves.

Freedom from an Irreversible Mistake

For those of us who do not have a permanent gift of singleness (i.e. contentment to stay single for life), our time as a soloist for Jesus can be a challenge . . . and some would say a trial. But the trial usually has hope of ending. I know this is easier said than done, but the decision to stay single is generally reversible. Once married, though, you are married. If you make a poor choice of life partner, you are stuck with that choice for better or for worse, until death do you part. The trial of marriage to an ungodly person has no exit strategy. And even the tragic event of the death of a spouse or a divorce usually makes life more difficult than before. This is why the Puritan Henry Smythe once said, "First a man must choose his love; then he must love his choice." Marriage is, by definition, irreversible.

To the married I give this charge (not I, but the Lord): the wife should not separate from her husband (but if she does, she should remain unmarried or else be reconciled to her husband), and the husband should not divorce his wife. To the rest I say (I, not the

Lord) that if any brother has a wife who is an unbeliever, and she consents to live with him, he should not divorce her. If any woman has a husband who is an unbeliever, and he consents to live with her, she should not divorce him.

—1 Corinthians 7:10–13

Consider the shock of the apostles when Jesus told them how serious marriage vows are (Matthew 19:9–11). When they understood how irreversible marriage is in God's eyes, the disciples responded with jaw-dropping incredulity and rightly figured it might be wise never to marry. Indeed, the only reason anyone should *not* wisely opt for singleness is because it is a gift of God's grace without which no one could be content to remain unmarried indefinitely. So during seasons of singleness, however long they may last, we must rest in God's grace. The season itself is a good gift.

The Network Safety Net

Everyone needs companionship and support, but the church has a special obligation to single people who have no other believers in their extended family. The church is a surrogate family that God has provided for those who are truly alone: it is "the household of God" (1 Timothy 3:15; 1 Peter 4:17), so we should act like a household. Paul specifically says that the church must care for widows who have no financial support from family (1 Timothy 5:3–5), but this wisdom can extend to the social and emotional support needed by all single people without believing family.

All single people in a church should feel like part of a family, and they should help create the kind of loving church culture that we need: "If you have good reasons for choosing to stay single—either temporarily or permanently—you need to be actively building a strong network of friendships in order to have the much-needed relational input and support of other people."[4] If you are unmarried in a church full of married people who only hang out with their married friends, don't wait for them to do what they ought. Reach out to them and help the church become what it is called to be.

The day after Shin A-Lam lost the silver medal and a chance at gold due to the time-keeping debacle described at the beginning of this chapter, the International Fencing Federation offered her a "special medal" as a consolation prize honoring her sportsmanship. Shin turned down the gesture and instead chose to focus on earning what she termed "a real medal" in the team event the following week. Sure enough, she and her two teammates secured silver for South Korea in the ladies team épée event.

Shin's exuberance was especially touching in light of what had transpired at the individual competition. It's not that she didn't care about that experience anymore, but she found genuine solace in belonging to her team and country, saying "My teammates and people back in [South] Korea gave me wonderful support this week."[5] Shin had learned a precious lesson that there is never a reason to *feel* alone when you are not alone. And in the church, nobody is alone.

Ask Yourself

1. If you are married, do you view single adults as "missing out" or as occupying a privileged position of potential ministry in God's church family? What passages bring biblical balance to your opinion?

2. If you are not married, what opportunities do you have for ministry or other blessings specifically because you are single? What areas of current ministry would become more difficult if/when you are married?

3. Craft a short response to insensitive or annoying comments you hear about singleness. Single people should prepare to answer graciously when accosted by well-intentioned married people. And married people should prepare to speak from a biblical worldview and challenge or inform others who may not have given much thought to God's view of singleness.

4. If you are single but desire to be married, what steps are you as a single person taking to be marriageable? Think about spiritual, financial, or even physical goals that would benefit you when God presents an opportunity to pursue a romantic relationship.

8

Team Supporters
Para-Family Support

Can you imagine a moderately successful athletic team without fans? You don't even expect an empty stadium for the worst team with the worst record. True fans show up no matter what the score, and they wear the team colors and sing all the cheers. Their very presence and enthusiasm helps the team play the game, even if they end up losing more than winning.

Somewhat similarly, para-church organizations come alongside local churches to help them accomplish their God-given tasks. They are the bridesmaids to Christ's Bride. For example, various mission agencies help small, financially challenged church bodies send missionaries overseas. The agencies may help raise finances, provide the experience needed to train and send the missionary, and oversee administrative work. Some churches can simply not perform all of this without outside help.

Problems arise, however, when people view parachurch organizations as substitutes for their local churches. Some believers don't serve in their church or give financially to their churches because they believe their work in and contribution to para-church ministries suffices as their Christian duty to participate in the Lord's work.

We see the same advantages and challenges to family-friendly helpers that I will call *para-family support*. God has designed various support systems to come alongside the family, and we should welcome them as such. Use these resources where needed. But remember that they are friends of the family, not actually part of the family structure. Parents must not palm off their spiritual responsibility to educate their children onto good para-family structures like the church Sunday school program, the youth group, or the local school. Doing so reveals overdependence on your team supporters. At the same time, some of these helpers view themselves as having a more significant role than what the Bible says they should have. Well-meaning grandparents can, for example, become far too involved in dispensing unsolicited parenting advice, marriage counseling, or financial support.

In this chapter, we will examine three common team supporters that families commonly use and misuse: schools, church programs, and older relatives/friends.

The School as Para-family Support

The typical loving, Christian parent has strong opinions about whether children should (or may) be schooled at home, at a private (Christian) school, or in the public school system. The way some proponents of the various views talk, you would think they're discussing whether to send their children to the heaven, purgatory, or hell of Dante's *Divine Comedy*. But I wonder why Christians feel as though they must passionately hold to any one of these options. We have three little kids (and counting), and I can already tell that each of them will thrive in different environments. I also believe that they all could, by God's grace, survive any of the usual school options.

Before you get excited, let me tell you now: the following words are not intended to help you choose the best school option for your child. Instead, they are meant to help you understand that however you school your children, that structure must not replace the family as the primary source of a child's spiritual formation, development, and practice. The school—whether public, private, or home-based—is simply a support for the family, not a replacement for it. Some families recognize their inadequacy in teaching their kids calculus and decide to staff that out to a local school. Other families seem to assume that homeschooling their children automatically achieves the biblical mandates for parental training. The method of schooling is an entirely different matter, however, from whether parents are truly involved in teaching their children about the Lord and training them to apply the Bible's wisdom to their lives.

The best I can do is remind you of what a school is *not*. Simply put, school is not family. Even the best school is not an institution that God recognizes as responsible for the spiritual education of children. Rather, God commands *parents* to teach their children about God. Schools may make that task more difficult, or they may facilitate it, but at no time may a parent assume that spiritual development is the responsibility of a school or curriculum.

It makes sense to me why a parent would get upset with a school that does a poor job at teaching a child trigonometry or English grammar. What are we paying them for if not to teach the students math that is over our heads? But a parent who becomes disgruntled at a school because its classrooms lack Bible instruction or wholesome morals or wise discussion of worldview has missed the point of school (and the point of this book). These things are the prerogative of the parent. It certainly is nice when a school helps with that, but it is not biblically their role.

Of course, homeschooling avoids schools as para-family. A team doesn't need fans to win (just look at the New York Mets), but any given family may have a plethora of legitimate reasons to avail themselves of the help a school offers. There is nothing sinful, for example, about parents who dropped out of high school admitting that they cannot keep up with their gifted eleventh-grader's chemistry syllabus. Meanwhile, even highly educated parents might outsource schooling as a way to be more involved in their local community. Parents must prayerfully determine God's will for each of their children and take care not to neglect the business God has given them as a family.

Parents don't have to be smart to be wise, and they don't need diplomas to be godly. But parents do need to do the best they can to equip their children spiritually for their intellectual education, no matter where it happens. Parents using the school as para-family support must still actively participate in their children's education.

So how can we use school, whether it happens in the home or outside the home, as a helper? How can we make sure that school has not become a substitute?

Spot the Mistakes

Parents should get to know the content of whatever curriculum their children are learning. Work as a team to spot inaccuracies in textbooks: ask your kids questions, encourage fact checking, and encircle their education with a robust biblical worldview. Also keep a keen ear for opinions taught as facts, especially about the course of history, the function of culture, and when life begins. Bring the Bible to bear on what your child hears and sees.

When teachers venture away from their subjects and begin to interpret the material in ways that have spiritual implications, they have drifted into spiritual education. Parents need to be very involved in these moments. School teachers are not your kids' pastors or parents, and you and your children need to understand that for the sake of loving instruction. As Paul warned Timothy,

> The aim of our charge is love that issues from a pure heart and a good conscience and a sincere faith. Certain persons, by swerving from these, have wandered away into vain discussion, desiring to be teachers of the law, without understanding either what they are saying or the things about which they make confident assertions.
> —1 Timothy 1:5–7

Do not hesitate to augment or even correct what teachers say to your children about spiritual matters. Know what is being taught and advocated in your children's classrooms. Get to know the teachers and frequently ask your children what they are learning.

Screen the Friends

Parents should be involved in the social influence that is part of the school experience. Friendships that develop around church and even through extended family gatherings do not tend to expose children to so many different religious backgrounds and worldviews as schools do. This can be a valuable opportunity to learn respect for others, but parents must manage it carefully and closely. As we have already discussed in earlier chapters, parents must bear in mind the biblical warning that "Bad company ruins good morals" (1 Corinthians 15:33).

Remember *Who's the Boss*

Do not allow a school to dictate your family's priorities. Teachers understandably view their particular subjects as important, and they may view their assignments and exams as more important than the time your family wishes to spend together. Even during my own days as a high school English teacher, I tried to convince parents that leaving for family vacation one day early before break might make their child miss an important test or lesson. Now, as a parent, I understand something that never occurred to me as a single man teaching high school: the parent does not work for the school, but the school works for the parent.

If our family attended every school-related event, we would have no time alone as a family. There is always a track meet needing spectators, a play requiring an audience, a club begging for parent assistance and child participation. Friends' parties and parent-teacher meetings and countless other activities of vital importance invade the precious space that is our family schedule like an aggressive cancer. So families need to close ranks against all the good things they could do through or around their schools. Insist instead on the good things you *must* do.

The school as para-family support should help, but not compete or interfere with the family. Children need to learn this from a young age, and parents need to remind themselves of this often. Parents may also need to have some "define the relationship" chats with teachers. And if a school situation becomes untenable due to unreasonable demands on your family's time and loyalties, it may be time to reconsider the education path your family has chosen. If your "define the relationship" chats do not yield positive results, you may need a breakup talk. Be as considerate as possible with the teachers serving your family, but also take your biblical responsibilities seriously and remember who works for whom.

The Church as Para-family Support

The mistake made in the relationship between the church and the family is usually made by parents. Schools often seem designed according to the principle that they bear the primary responsibility for molding your children, but Christian parents unblinkingly saddle churches with this misallocation. Think about it: churches only have access to children for short and relatively infrequent bursts of time (Sunday school for an hour weekly, youth group for a couple of hours weekly, and perhaps the odd youth camp or vacation Bible school). Yet many parents palm off on the church the responsibility to teach and disciple their children in spiritual matters.

I know of unbelieving parents who drop their children off at a local church Sunday school class and then go out for breakfast. They think they are doing a great thing by providing their children with spiritual nourishment. But that is like feeding the kids vegetables once a week and chocolate cake for every other meal. We see a more moderate version of this attitude in Christian parents who compartmentalize their weeks into a secular Monday to Saturday with a sacred Sunday. The home has no Bible teaching, no intentional discipleship, no shepherding conversations. Life is lived apart from God except for rushed mealtime or bedtime prayers.

If you asked these parents whether they believe spiritual education and discipleship is important, they would likely answer, "Yes, of course! The Bible commands it, which is why we never let our kids miss church or youth group." These types of parents treat the church like a substitute player rather than a supporter. They want the church to function as a spiritual surrogate parent to the child while the real parent is all but absent from the soul shepherding.

In the previous two chapters we saw some of what daily, life-on-life discipleship looks like for kids in the little and minor leagues, so here we must remember that the Bible always instructs *parents*, not the church, to train their own children in the ways of God (see Deuteronomy 6:4–9; Ephesians 6:4). Parents need to know what their children are hearing at Sunday school and youth group, and they need to understand the youth workers' views on various ethical and theological matters. Parents need to think about how the kids' training at church matches what the family learns and practices at home. It's a serious matter (see Matthew 18:5–6). More than anything, children need to see modeled and fleshed out at home what they are learning at church.

The church is an important part of para-family support, so parents need to instill in their children a love and respect for the church and its leadership. Attend corporate worship and other church functions regularly, and make a commitment never to badmouth church leaders in front of your children. But the best way to let the church operate as an effective family supporter and to cultivate in your children respect for the church is simply to strive, by God's grace, to practice and teach at home what you hear preached and taught at church.

"Senior Saints" as Para-family Support

It takes a lifetime of sustained training and experience to attain Ninth Duan, the highest martial arts rank in China, but most people earn it at a younger age than Lu Zijian did. Born in China in 1893, Zijian developed a love for various Chinese martial arts and eventually pursued competitive fighting, not winning his first significant gold medal until 1911 at the age of 28. His notoriety grew rapidly when he killed a well-known Japanese boxer with a single blow from the palm of his hand, and in 2002, at the ripe age of 109, Zijian achieved Ninth Duan. Even at age 116, the spritely supercentenarian was still immersed in the world of martial arts, actively participating in competitions and widely sought after as an instructor. Zijian eventually died on February 20, 2012, after 118 years and 128 days of life (once you pass 110, every day is a birthday).

People like Zijian make me want to have a long-term perspective of my life. Just think if he had retired in his sixties! When most people's vitality begins winding down, that fit octogenarian had just gotten warmed up. I find that in the church, some older saints are like Zijian—they have irrepressible energy and contagious *joie de vivre*. Others have a bleak outlook on the impending autumn of their lives, perhaps because life's disappointments and trials take different tolls on people. Indeed, the Scriptures present with unvarnished realism the physical troubles that accompany aging (Ecclesiastes 12:1–8). But the Bible also admonishes us to be good stewards of our life experience and the wisdom that comes only with age. Psalm 92:12–15 stands in stark contrast to the "planned obsolescence" of our world's modern retirement mindset:

> The righteous flourish like the palm tree
> and grow like a cedar in Lebanon.
> They are planted in the house of the LORD;
> they flourish in the courts of our God.
> They still bear fruit in old age;
> they are ever full of sap and green,
> to declare that the LORD is upright;
> he is my rock, and there is no unrighteousness in him.

Jay Adams writes of this passage,

> God's attitude, as it normally does, conflicts sharply with that of the world. An older green tree, thriving and producing fruit, is hardly one that you would uproot and replace with a younger one. It seems that God expects the righteous to lead a vital, useful life among his fellow believers no matter what his age.[1]

People with real life experience have much more credibility when they proclaim the goodness and faithfulness of God. Consider the power of this statement coming from an aged David: "I have been young, and now am old, yet I have not seen the righteous forsaken or his children begging for bread" (Psalm 37:25). Younger parents need older saints—grandparents but also individuals and families with even just a little more experience than they—to come alongside them as they fulfill God's will for them as a family. These "senior saints" may provide wisdom and sometimes even financial support for younger families pursuing God's glory.

Wisdom Support without Becoming Overbearing

The Bible unabashedly extols the virtue of age because experience (represented by "gray hair" in Proverbs 16:31 and 20:29) generally yields understanding. In fact, God gives the gift of wisdom to older people *so that* they can share their wisdom with younger generations. In Titus 2:2–5, Paul assumes that younger people lack the knowledge and experience that older people have, so he encourages the more mature believers to teach and train and set an example for younger people. Those in the church who have been blessed with many years should occupy themselves with passing down wisdom in this way. As the psalmist proclaims,

> O God, from my youth you have taught me,
>   and I still proclaim your wondrous deeds.
>   So even to old age and gray hairs,
>   O God, do not forsake me,
>   until I proclaim your might to another generation,
>   your power to all those to come.
> —Psalm 71:17–18

Of course, giving counsel requires real wisdom, not merely experience or self-declared know-how. We might think of the proverbial sticky wicket of a mother-in-law advising her daughter-in-law, or the tricky reality that "the way we did things back then" may not actually be biblically wise. These kinds of conversations can become sources of contention between the generations. Parents of married couples especially must remember and respect God's "leave and cleave" principle from Genesis 2: the new husband and wife are a new and distinct family before God, and they have their own responsibilities and authority structure. The young family is not merely another branch on a family tree but a new sapling that is its own unit even as it needs support to grow.

Financial Support without Enabling Overdependence

I once noticed a gray-haired man and woman hauling a boat trailer sporting a bumper sticker that cheerfully declared, "I'm spending my children's inheritance." I get the joke, but I also feel sympathy for the couple's kids. The attitude that "This is my money that I have earned for my enjoyment" misses the biblical truth that all wealth is a gift from God to be used for God's purposes. Yes, one reason God gives wealth is that we would enjoy it to his glory, but he also means for us to meet the needs of others. This is especially true within families (see 1 Timothy 5:8).

Most parents possess a financial advantage and stability that their fledglings don't yet have. So God thinks it a virtue to use your wealth to help establish your children: "A good man leaves an inheritance to his children's children, but the sinner's wealth is laid up for the righteous" (Proverbs 13:22). Even before the time of "inheritance" comes, parents ought to provide financial and other physical support if they can and if it seems wise to do so. Remember that when Paul assured the Corinthians—whom he considered his spiritual children—that he would not be a financial burden on them, he noted how normal it is for parents to bless their children financially (2 Corinthians 12:14).

I do not mean to imply that it is healthy to provide ongoing support enabling a wealthier lifestyle than your grown children can afford on their own. This can beget laziness and overdependence. But wise parents might provide occasional assistance with purchases that help establish their children's families for the long term. I know of parents who established mutual fund accounts for their children when they were born, contributing monthly throughout their lives to pay for college tuition when the time came. These parents were not wealthy, but they set aside a small amount every month for something they believed would help establish their children in good careers. When their children earned enough scholarship to pay their own way through college, those mutual fund accounts waited to become down payments on houses. Now as grandparents, that same couple is establishing mutual funds for their grandchildren. After all, "House and wealth are inherited from fathers" (Proverbs 19:14).

The Gift of Loyal Fans

There was more at stake than a mere trophy and bragging rights in the 1995 Rugby World Cup. The first time that South Africa had even competed since sanctions against apartheid had forbid it, the country also had the honor of hosting the tournament. That was actually the only way to ensure that the underdog team would even qualify, though getting past the first round would prove challenging for a team without crucial international exposure for so many years. Astonishingly, the South African Springboks made it to the finals and faced the New Zealand All Blacks, their historical rival.

South Africa had recently held their first-ever democratic elections after ousting the oppressive and racist apartheid regime with surprising calm. Tensions were high as the new government considered changing the national emblem, the flag, the national sporting colors (green and gold), and even the country's name. During these turbulent times, civil peace seemed fragile. Then came the Rugby World Cup.

Rugby had essentially been the national sport of the overthrown government. Black people had not been permitted to play the sport competitively, and they naturally associated rugby with white oppression. But the newly elected President Nelson Mandela magnanimously called upon the citizens of all political outlooks and cultural heritages to support the national rugby team, thus putting harmful stereotypes and factious allegiances behind them. Mandela attended the final game himself and wore a rugby jersey with the team captain's number. He wished to set an example of national solidarity by supporting this formerly "whites only" sport. The gesture won the hearts of all the people.

The Springboks played remarkably well that day against the All Blacks—formidable opponents and clear favorites to win the championship. When the nail-biting game tied at full-time, it forced the first overtime in World Cup final history. Then, thirty-two minutes into the extra time, the score still tied at 12–12, South Africa's Joel Stransky launched a spectacular 30-meter drop kick to score the three points that secured a 15–12 victory for the Springboks.

I remember watching that moment on television in Pretoria. The 63,000 fans in the stadium went wild, and countless home viewers streamed into the streets, screaming and crying while cars honked raucously for hours all over the country. In an on-field interview just after the game, a reporter had asked an understandably emotional team captain, François Piennaar, how it felt to have the support of all those fans in the stadium. Piennaar famously corrected him: "We did not have 63,000 fans behind us today; we had 43 million South Africans." Indeed, it was a moment of unprecedented national celebration.

No athlete can quantify the value of loyal and enthusiastic team supporters, but they are essential. The same can be said for Christian families blessed with a God-given network of supporters. God has designed families to need and rely on the relational support of others. While not substitutes for the family structure God has ordained, the para-family community plays a significant supporting role. Parents need good cheerleaders as they pursue the goal of glorifying God though their families.

Ask Yourself

1. List the specific supporters God has brought into your life that could benefit your family (e.g., schools, grandparents, people in the church). Thank God for the many supporters he has made available.

2. Do you neglect these supporters as a resource to provide the help God wants to give you? Or do you perhaps rely too much on some of them?

3. If you are a grandparent, do you make yourself available to help? If you do, are you "present" without becoming overbearing or insistent about the "right way" to parent? How can you better fulfill your supporting role?

4. If your family is not blessed with close and godly grandparents, consider approaching a godly older couple in the church to help you meet needs.

9

Team Huddle

The Family that Prays Together

Sometimes, coaches and quarterbacks devise unique signals that opposing teams cannot easily decipher, but what if a football team needed to use codified sign language to discuss plays and receive tactical instructions? The disadvantage of such communication is that any sign-savvy peeping Tom, Dick, or Harry in view can eavesdrop on your conversation. This may not be a common hurdle in football, but the all-deaf football team at Gallaudet University had to jump it.

During a crucial game in 1889, Gallaudet got frustrated because an opponent who could sign kept "overhearing" their plays. Quarterback Paul Hubbard resourcefully engineered a simple but historic solution: the team huddle. His teammates gathered in a tight circle, bent forward with their backs to the would-be spies, and thus enjoyed the privacy and camaraderie of an intimate planning session. The huddle was so effective that it soon became standard practice for all football teams.

There is a clear parallel between the role the huddle plays in team sports and the spiritual regrouping that takes place in family devotions. In both instances, the players physically draw near to one another so that they can communicate simply and clearly. The team captain takes the lead, drawing the other players close to protect them from outside noise and to direct the conversation. In the huddle, the team makes plans, and players also encourage one another. This time is generally for members only—a safe place to share sensitive matters. It's also the place to celebrate wins or mourn losses.

Christianity is a team sport—no way of getting around that. Community is integral to the very fabric of Christian worship. Local churches exist to fulfill God's commands in a way that brings blessing to the church and radiates a testimony of light in a dark world: "By this all people will know that you are my disciples, if you have love for one another" (John 13:35). We *cannot* live the Christian life well as spiritual hermits, but need the community of the church. Likewise, the family must operate as a collective unit. The family, after all, is a microcosm of the covenant community.

Think of the many commands God gives believers that they cannot obey in isolation. The family is a great place to practice many "one another" commands given to congregations:

- Comfort and agree with one another (2 Corinthians 13:11).
- Bear one another's burdens (Galatians 6:2).
- Bear with one another (Ephesians 4:2).
- Speak truth to one another (Ephesians 4:25).
- Be kind and forgive one another (Ephesians 4:32).
- Sing psalms, hymns, and spiritual songs to one another (Ephesians 5:19).
- Submit to one another (Ephesians 5:21).
- Admonish one another (Colossians 3:16).
- Love one another (1 Thessalonians 3:12).
- Encourage one another (1 Thessalonians 4:18).
- Exhort one another (Hebrews 3:13).
- Think about how to stir one another up to love and good deeds (Hebrews 10:24).
- Use your gifts to serve one another (1 Peter 4:10).

Family unity flows out from redeemed hearts as normal Christian behavior. Where better to rehearse God-honoring actions and attitudes than in one's home?

Regularity

The tug-of-war between childrens' school activities and parents' work schedules, along with the all the usual demands of life, can incrementally edge out family time. In our day, it is in vogue to demote "quantity time" to the consolation prize "quality time." But can mere nanoseconds of bonding actually compensate for hours and days of laconic, cursory interaction? When family time gets relegated to something sporadic rather than regular, we declare that family relationships are incidental to our real commitments of school and work and other individual pursuits.

Reorganizing your priorities will require intentionality. You might begin by scheduling a regular family meeting, whether daily, three times a week, or weekly. Do not focus the time on activity, as in a weekly "game night" or a monthly picnic, but on relationship. Families need fun bonding times, but spiritual regrouping is too important to lump with various amusing activities. So build into your family ethos and practice a regular family worship time. I call this the "team huddle." A regular, planned time with a spiritual agenda has myriad benefits, but here are a few to consider:

- Regular family worship gives parents an opportunity to diagnose where their children are spiritually. Sometimes, kids have doubts and questions that they are embarrassed to share with spiritual leaders or parents. The family huddle can become a place where children feel safe to freely discuss various spiritual topics.

- Family worship gives every member of the family various models for structured times of prayer and devotional practice. Many adult Christians have no idea how to spend time with the Lord in a devotional way. They know they should read their Bible, pray, and worship, but they have only seen this done in church. Children should grow up seeing their dad and mom praying out loud, enjoying Scripture, and applying it to daily situations. This habit is more effectively caught than taught.

- Family worship creates a general family environment where it is normal and comfortable to talk about spiritual matters and one's relationship with the Lord. In some families, bringing God into a discussion feels odd because it happens so irregularly. But when talking about Jesus is a daily family event, it feels natural to make him part of other discussions too. You don't want to become a family that only hears what the Bible says in context of discipline and punishment. God's Word should permeate our lives and relationships at all times. Family worship times promote this culture in the home.

- Regular family worship facilitates an ongoing alertness to answered prayers, which instills deeper faith in God. Corporate prayer is not just about modeling: it actually works (see James 5:13–18)!

The Bible provides no template for family meetings, but it does give families some essential principles that can shape their regular gatherings. Parents must have a united front regarding how they discipline, counsel, and educate their children (see the Genesis 2 mandate to operate as "one flesh"). As we have discussed before, children need their *parents* to instruct them, nurture them in the Word of God, and hold them accountable (see Deuteronomy 6:4–9 and Ephesians 6:1). Other teachers are great, but a child's primary discipleship should come first and foremost from the *parents*. Build such instruction into the daily routines of life (see Deuteronomy 6:4–9). And make sure that what you teach is biblically accurate and profitable, not moralistic platitudes (see Mark 9:42).

Families are not designed to operate effectively apart from God's grace (John 15:5). The Holy Spirit alone changes attitudes, shapes behavior, and brings wisdom and guidance to challenging situations in life. Children whose parents pray with them about situations that matter to them gain over time a growing catalogue of answered prayer. This boosts the faith of children and teaches them to rely on the Spirit for help when they are on their own outside the huddle. Remember the goal of parenting: to raise children who are independently dependent on Christ.

Resources

All you really need for family worship is the Bible. Simply read to your children from God's Word. Parents leading family worship usually know more than their kids do about the Lord, and they may be tempted to tell Bible stories from memory rather than actually read them from a Bible, but this may lead to perpetuating common tiny inaccuracies. For example, did Elijah go to heaven in a chariot of fire or a whirlwind? Did David kill Goliath with a sling or a sword? Most children get these questions wrong because their parents have unwittingly abridged the biblical accounts. Also, opening the Bible and reading aloud from it makes a vivid statement to your children. As soon as they are old enough to read aloud, you should encourage them to read the Bible to each other.

Children's Bibles

You may have a particular translation of the Bible that you prefer for your own personal study, but remember that if you have children, family devotion time must benefit them. Hopefully, you as a believer are having your own individual devotional time with the Lord, at which time you should use whatever tool suits your own needs. But when you are with the kids, use a version of the Bible that offers vocabulary they can understand.

- The Good News Bible deliberately uses a limited number of English words to facilitate understanding by children and second-language readers.
- The New International Version is suitable for early teens.
- The English Standard Version, New King James, and New American Standard Bible are all good for close study—per-

fect for teenagers and older children who have a good grasp of English.

If your children are still very young (just learning to talk or otherwise unable to read), they are not too young to get in the habit of opening a book and making observations from it. A well-illustrated, colorful, age-appropriate Bible can prove helpful to engage illiterate children. Ask questions about what they see in the pictures, and then explain the content behind the illustrations. One of our family favorites is David R. Helm's *The Big Picture Bible*, which emphasizes Christocentricity throughout the Scriptures alongside Gail Shoonmaker's stunning watercolor illustrations. We also use Sally Lloyd-Jones' *Jesus Storybook Bible* and Marty Machowski's *The Gospel Story Bible* along with a couple of others. Alternating between different Bibles keeps the time fresh and interesting for children, and it helps them see that there are different versions of the Bible—a valuable lesson for later understanding.

When looking for children's Bibles, I hunt for versions that include lesser-known passages like the stories of Naboth's vineyard and the Witch of Endor. I usually check the flood story in Genesis 6 to see what the translation offers as the reason why God wiped out the world. Some say, "To clean the planet." Yuck. If it says to wipe out wickedness, then we're cooking. If the New Testament translation says that Jesus died to leave us an example, I fill in the lacking content myself: yes, to leave us an example *and* to bear the Father's wrath and atone for the sins of the world, including this family and you personally. Kids can handle hard truths and heavy theology if explained clearly.

Catechism

Family worship is not a new thing; families have been having devotions together for centuries, which means we contemporary folks are blessed to have many resources to assist us. One time-honored tradition that many families have found very effective for training children is the catechism approach where children are asked questions and taught to memorize answers.

- We teach our four-year-old an abridged children's version of the Westminster Catechism. Brian Stone's *Teach Your Family the Truth* has 112 questions designed well with a question and answer per page as well as prompts for discussion, further reading, and singing.
- For school-aged children and teenagers, I recommend Dennis Hustedt's *Grounded in God's Word*, which explains the Scriptural basis for the doctrine being taught, also with devotional prompts. *A Catechism for Boys and Girls* from Reformation Today Trust is another good resource: easy-to-use, 29 pages (free online at http://www.reformedreader. org/ccc/acbg.htm) with 133 questions and brief answers.

Catechizing capitalizes on the sponginess of young minds. The younger we are, the more our brains absorb information. That's why tech-savvy seven-year-olds can teach their intimidated grandparents how to use the latest touch-screen gadgets. What better knowledge to feed that eagerness than the truth of God's Word?

Roles, or How My Wife Helped Me "Man Up" and Lead Family Devotionals

I must confess that I did not always see the benefit of a family devotion time. Or more accurately, I chose not to consider it because I'm a slacker. There is no other explanation. This was an area in which my wife fulfilled her God-appointed role as helper by prying me out of the La-Z-Boy recliner of my complacency.

You see, things were going well for my life plan, and I guess I figured the next thing on my checklist would eventually come on its own. Throughout my single years, I had pined and prayed for a dream life that looked like an idyllic hybrid of Thomas Kinkade meets *Cheaper by the Dozen*. My checklist didn't seem too much to ask:

- One beautiful wife, preferably from California. This prayer was shallow, immature, and embarrassingly Beach Boys, I know. But God said yes anyway. So, check.
- One huddle of doting children. Check, check, and check again (so far).
- One Wheaten labrador named Spurgeon, so that even the worst workday would be accompanied by a cheerful, happy grin. Check.
- A family full of Archers glorifying God and enjoying him together. Er, no check yet. Not exactly.

In the IMAX theater of my mind's eye, we would pursue that final checkmark during calm and cherubic family devotion scenes. My little flock would nestle at my feet as I expounded God's Word, Bible on lap, like a daddy bird dropping juicy spiritual truths into the cheeping mouths of eager little minds. But for quite a while, evenings in the Archer home looked less like a Kinkade painting and more like CNN news clips of hurricane damage. Devos got drowned in a swirling flood of kid things: diaper change > bath > PJs > spaghetti dinner > bath again > clean PJs > bedtime milk > spill > more clean PJs > drive-by prayers with summarized Samson stories as Daddy rushes out to teach a "real Bible study" to his "other flock."

Why was this our evening routine? Because I'm a slacker. My spineless lack of discipline was the only problem. Not the spilled milk or spaghetti (though we did learn not to do bath before dinner).

Then one day God said "Enough." No visions or dreams or angels. God used my wife to graciously and patiently help me recalibrate my priorities. She did it without nagging like a dripping tap, which in China and Proverbs is recognized as a cruel torture technique. She did it without subtle hints, as if playing silent marriage charades. She did it without making me feel like a slacker, though I was being one. She simply found a time outside the busy moments of life, made a date, brewed some condensed milk coffee, and then asked if I would be okay with her telling the kids that each night after dinner and bath but before bedtime, part of the new routine would include family worship. The Holy Spirit did the rest.

We are not there yet. But we are edging closer than we were before.

Coaching Corner: Husbands

Husbands, this is actually your job. It is the man's prerogative and privilege to lead his family in their spiritual growth. Your wife is your helper fit specifically for you, and God uses her to help accomplish this plan, but he has not designed her to lead this effort. One way God may have your wife "help" you is through rebuke or encouragement if you consistently fumble the ball by neglecting to lead as you should, so do not resent her for hinting, asking, or even nagging that you lead family devotions: if you would do what God has designed you to do, she wouldn't need to say anything. Rather, take her efforts as a reminder from God of your responsibility. And then get on with it.

Coaching Corner: Wives

Some women pray and graciously request that their husbands lead the family spiritually. And when that doesn't work, they begin leaving cryptic clues in late-night chats, finally resigned to take the lead themselves in their children's spiritual training. If your husband is not a believer, you will need to lead your children in their spiritual walk with the Lord. Seek counsel from your pastor on how to do this in a way that does not cause tension in your marriage. Even a believing husband can begin to feel like a loser with such a wife. Granted, he may well be disobeying God's command to lead his family, but feeling like a loser doesn't encourage change.

Ladies, if your husband knows you consider him to be a spineless spiritual jellyfish, he may act even more like one. Most men want to make their wives proud of them, but if they feel like they can't ever win, they will lose heart. Do you respect your husband as your husband (Ephesians 5:33), even if he doesn't act like you think he should all of the time? If you do, you will use encouraging words as a balm to energize his conscience.

You might help with practical suggestions, like how to find a regular time for family worship. Kids thrive on routine, like little Pavlovian pets, but so do grown-ups. If your husband is a believer and you guard the routine, the rest might just fall into place without any water-torture techniques or psychological warfare.

Coaching Corner: Kids

If you have not grown up with regular family worship and your parents suddenly attempt to bring such spiritual leadership into your family routine, your job is to make that herculean task a bit more manageable through respectful participation. Don't complain, roll your eyes, sulk, or otherwise make the hill they are climbing steeper. God promises you that if you honor your parents in the Lord (i.e., honor them in their godly pursuits) you will reap blessing.

One Way to Skin a Devotional Cat

Honestly, I felt embarrassed to need my wife's help in leading my family spiritually, but as with the lady speaking through our GPS unit, I slowly learned not to argue with the voice of reason. That said, let me issue this vital disclaimer: I am no expert. I seriously had little to no idea what I was doing during family worship. We have only been at this for a few years, but by God's grace, the discipline has been pretty consistent. Now our kids love family worship. They ask for it. That can't be bad, right?

Keep at it, and you will find the right routine for your family. But I will offer here what we do, which may be of some help.

1. CARVE THE TIME INTO YOUR ROUTINE.

Routine has been the key to our consistency. I need this as much as the kids do. Every night after bath and before bedtime, our entire family gathers at the same place, our living room couch. The children have come to expect this and often prompt me as I'm deliberating whether to use the precious "exception clause" for when I'm exhausted. As it turns out, their beaming expectant faces cure all fatigue. Instead, we make exceptions only on the rare nights when

I must go somewhere before the kids' bedtime, and even then, my wife fills in that gap.

2. Read the Bible.

Because our children are very young, we start with reading a short story from a children's Bible. I try to be expressive and funny with lots of voices and accents, and sometimes we do some role-play or I ask them to guess the next step. As they get older, this may become more content-driven and less attention-keeping, but fun is a core ingredient. No one wants to think of devotion time as a chore or a hoop to jump through.

This is also the time you would introduce the kids to a catechism curriculum if you so choose. Children can usually memorize Scripture and catechism answers at a rate that puts their parents to shame. Use this spongy phase to give your kids truth tools that they will use for the rest of their lives.

3. Apply what you have read.

Dad should draw one or two applications out of the lesson that can be understood and put into practice in the life of the family. Help your family respond and not merely hear (James 1:22). If you skip this step, you miss an opportunity to show that love for God always leads to obedience (1 John 2:3). I do this by asking some simple either/or questions that start, "Do we learn," to encourage my children to think. I might ask, "Do we learn that God doesn't mind our sin, or do we learn that God hates sin and wants to punish it?" For my older boy (age six), I ask questions that probe deeper, and I have been repeatedly blown away by his comprehension.

Of course, your kids will probably start asking questions that naturally lead to application. Kids aren't just hard drives; they are processors. They don't just want memory work; they require understanding. One of my young ones once responded, "But if God hardened Pharaoh's heart, why didn't he un-harden it and give faith to the Egyptians to also trust in the Passover Lamb?" Er, I hadn't planned on discussing the doctrine of unconditional election. Yikes. "You'll learn about that in the third year of seminary," I said. Another time, my four-year-old daughter asked, "If Jesus is holier than the ark of the covenant, why could people touch Jesus, but not the ark?" My answer: "Umm, ask your mother."

4. PRAY.

It's a cliché for a reason: the family that prays together usually *does* stay together. Experience proves that regular prayer with each other and for each other can be one of the most edifying and unifying family practices. Perhaps that's why Paul puts joy, prayer, and thanks together in 1 Thessalonians 5:16–18, knowing that God desires all three continually in his children.

Our family takes turns praying, first thanking God for one gift he has given our family and then asking him to meet one need that someone else in the family has. If one of the kids shares a need or burden, we let a sibling pray for that need. We use a simple template for prayer to make sure we cover all the bases. We don't do all of these every time we pray together, but over the course of a week, we make sure each child does each of these aspects of prayer at least once:

- Praise for who God is (i.e., celebrating God's attributes/nature).
- Confession (i.e., naming specific sins you committed that day/week or are currently struggling with).
- Petition (i.e., asking God to meet your own spiritual and physical needs and desires).
- Intercession (i.e., asking God to meet others' spiritual and physical needs and desires).
- Thanksgiving (i.e., thanking God for what he has done in history and in your life).

5. SING.

Kids often love singing more than their parents do, and good songs with solid truth can equip your children with a memorized cheat sheet of rich theology. As a family, we sing a song or two or three every night. We try to teach them a song they hear in church: we sing it every night for a week or so to help them learn it. We will also sing another song they already know. We always take requests and try to do a kid song with actions, which encourages participation and fun.

Use Colossians 3:16 as your guide: "Let the word of Christ dwell in you richly, teaching and admonishing one another in all wisdom, singing psalms and hymns and spiritual songs, with thankfulness in your hearts to God." Singing psalms to modern tunes can help kids (and parents) memorize Scripture. Singing hymns that contain great doctrines can help children understand and rejoice in deep truth that will stay them throughout their lives. Explain tricky words and concepts, and don't underestimate your children's ability to memorize and understand good theological hymns. Then sing other spiritual songs with catchy melodies to serve as ammunition for praise when your hearts feel expressive toward God.

6. END.

We keep family worship short. Seriously, this can make or break it. Ten or fifteen minutes fly quickly with singing, praying, and reading. You can always increase the time as your family grows into the discipline and your children get older, but on the whole, regularity is more important than length of time for family devotions. If the kids are gnawing at their wrists to end the misery of your dense, forty-five-minute exposition, you know you're making no impact.

Especially with young children, you should try to keep things light with a fun and expressive tone. Do not avoid somber subject matter: when we discuss the crucifixion, we are serious. But try to end every family worship time on a hopeful, joyful note.

Finally, mix things up so that the liturgy never becomes rote. We use the same Bible for a few nights in a row and then change to another one, rotating through four. We sometimes sing first rather than pray. You get the idea. There are a zillion ways to skin the devotional cat, and these are just some suggestions. You as a family must find your own rhythm, making sure to mind the biblical principles that are actually biblical: dads, lead the home, and parents, train your children.

Ask Yourself

1. What does your family currently do for family devotions? Who initiates each time, and who leads? How consistent are those times? What material do you use? Is the time long enough to be profitable but not so long that it becomes boring and a chore? Do you sing? Do you think your children enjoy it (or would enjoy it)? How could you adapt your family devotions to their levels of maturity and interest? What can you do to improve the quality and profitability of the time?

2. Fathers, can you think of ways that you can become more involved, proactive, and disciplined in family devotions? How can you improve as initiator and leader, and how can you ensure consistency in devotions? Enlist your wife's help in reminding or encouraging you, but be sure the family knows this is something *you* value.

3. If you are a wife whose husband does not lead family devotions, can you think of ways to encourage and remind him without nagging or condescending? You might think of a way to share privately with your husband how much this means to you, and ask respectfully if you can prepare a plan for him to use.

Conclusion

Rating Greatness

Our society is unblushingly results oriented. We rate greatness in sports by facts and figures, stats and times. We extol achievers whose performance can be proven by these objective evaluations. But deep down we all know that the way you race is more important than the result. Lance Armstrong's indomitable performance in the Tour de France cycle race secured him an unmatched seven winning titles. But when he finally confessed to using illegal performance enhancing substances throughout his career, Armstrong's legendary accomplishments were forever tarnished by the scandal. The unethical way in which he raced proved more important to his supporters than the impressive times he clocked.

Contrast that disappointing debacle with the inspiring achievement of the Tanzanian marathon runner John Stephen Akhwari. He placed dead last in the 1968 Olympic marathon in Mexico City, entering the stadium a full hour after the race had been won—a result that would never have warranted a mention in the news, according to the objective, stop-watched way we judge success in a marathon. But Akhwari's performance in that event made front-page news and has become a staple illustration for motivational speakers ever since. You see, Akhwari had stumbled badly earlier in the 26.2-mile race and had torn open his leg. The time he lost by dressing the injury, not to mention the agony of the wound itself, justified quitting the marathon, if only to seek proper medical attention. But the tenacious Tanzanian ran every step of that race.

As Akhwari limped doggedly into the stadium, he received a thunderous ovation. When he finally crossed the finish line a reporter gave him an opportunity to articulate what his actions had already declared. "Why didn't you give up?" the reporter asked. Akhwari replied that his country didn't send him to start the race but to finish it. Indeed, his faithfulness to finish mattered most.

So too, God rates greatness according to faithfulness, not achievement. This is why Paul dismissed human approval, regarding himself merely as a servant sent to do the work God gave him to do (1 Corinthians 4:2–3). Some couples boast of the number of years they have been married even if their relationship bears no resemblance to the portrait of Christ's love for his bride. Many rate their parenting skills by the material prosperity of their grown children. But when families compare themselves to other families or to some other movable criteria, they risk missing the whole point of the family. Success is not about what your family has achieved in measurable terms. God is far more concerned with how you relate to your family, how you view your priorities, and how you deal with challenges. Again, in a word, God is concerned with faithfulness.

Let's be honest. A self-righteous culture thrives among Christians with a biblical worldview: we tend to take pride in our so-called biblical techniques, and we are tempted to look down on parents whose out-of-control offspring appear inferior to our exemplary final products. But that's far from scriptural. Players must do their best within the rules to achieve the goal, but the best that Christians can do is faithfulness. The rules of the game are whatever God has outlined in his Word, and the goal is always to please our Lord (2 Corinthians 5:9).

Stay Faithful

Whenever we talk about family matters, Christians usually feel convicted that they fall short in some or most areas. After all, God's standard of perfection is understandably daunting. But this realization drives us to repent of our self-reliance and cling to God's grace in every situation that crops up in our family. You will experience many besetting challenges in this broken world, but don't fall into despair: God does not require perfection but instead only requires you to do the best you can with what you have been given.

Consider the parable of the talents (Matthew 25:14–30) in which Jesus taught that it doesn't matter what you have so much as whether you are faithful in what you have been given. You may be a single parent, divorced, widowed, or you may be married to an unbeliever; you may have children who are unbelievers and have rebelled. God only requires you to do the best you can by his grace. The results are entirely up to him, so they are, in a sense, incidental. The relationship of trust and obedience you have with him brings him glory. Faithfulness is at the heart of all we do for God (1 Corinthians 4:2).

Stay in Bounds

Part of being faithful is to trust that God's ways are better than whatever fortune-cookie wisdom the world is offering this season. The Bible is profitable for teaching, reproof, and training in righteousness (2 Timothy 3:16), and thus remains the best playbook for your family. How else will you know what to do and how to do it for God's glory?

When all family members play their positions, God gets glory from the way you trust in him together. Husbands, master the material God provides on loving your wife, leading your family, and training your children. Wives, trust that God will honor your commitment to submit to your husband's godly leadership. Parents, strive to instill in your children the values that God says are important, and as they mature, train them to be independently dependent on Christ. Children, cling to God's promise that he will bless you for obeying your parents. Single adults, use your God-given time and freedoms to invest in eternity, help other families, and enjoy being complete in Christ. Families, use whatever support systems God provides, but keep the para-family helps in their appropriate places.

God is glorified when we trust in his design and enjoy the blessings inherent to obedience. He sets the boundary lines in appropriate, pleasant places (Psalm 16:6). Seek his wisdom for your family and walk in it.

Stay Focused

If you want to remain motivated to seek God's will for your family, stay focused on the real goal, which is pleasing God. In the chaos of life, the short-range targets can easily obscure the ultimate goal. Parents start measuring their efforts by how clean the kids' rooms stay, how polite they are, and whether teachers compliment their good behavior. Husbands devalue the importance of leading their families. Moms get discouraged by how the house only stays tidy during the kids' naptimes.

When we lose focus on what is important to God, we risk missing the point of why our families exist. This leads to discouragement and frustration, or else seasons of excellence quickly move to feelings of self-righteousness. But most commonly, when the goal gets obscured, we lose all hope of success. That's what happened to the celebrated open-water swimmer Florence Chadwick.

On August 8, 1950, Florence Chadwick broke the world record for swimming the most formidable open-water challenge ever attempted—the English Channel. She covered 20 miles from France to England in an impressive 13 hours and 20 minutes. The following year, she did the swim again from England in 16 hours and 22 minutes, making history as the first woman to swim the Channel in both directions. (The increased time was due to tides and currents, not—as one reporter joked—because the swim was uphill.)

With this achievement behind her, Chadwick set her sites on a new goal for the following year: she would swim from Catalina Island to the Californian coast. But her 26-mile endeavor was complicated by particularly choppy conditions and a dense fog that set in after 15 hours of swimming. Chadwick persevered for 16 hours but suddenly gave up, mentally drained and physically exhausted. After being hauled into the boat, she discovered that she was less than a mile from the shore.

Chadwick later told a newspaper reporter that if she could have seen the land, she thought she could have made it. Her theory was proven in an unlikely way when she attempted the crossing again two months later. That time, when the same impenetrable fog descended on her, cloaking the destination, Chadwick made a concerted effort to visualize the shoreline. Fixed on her goal, she had the motivation she needed to complete the feat, even breaking the men's record by a gobsmacking two hours.

Never underestimate the hope that stems from focusing on your goal. Fixed on the right purpose, you will find yourself energized to move forward. And with a goal as noble as God's glory, we can be assured that God's grace will be with us, even through the most choppy waters of life.

Epilogue

Practice Makes Perfect

It started as a dare. Timothy Ferriss was dared by a friend to enter a Chinese kickboxing tournament (if you have friends like that, I hope you have good medical insurance), and Ferriss became a kickboxing champion overnight. What did he call the secret of his success? He said it wasn't physical talent:

> In 1999, sometime after quitting my second unfulfilling job and eating peanut-butter sandwiches for comfort, I won the gold medal at the Chinese Kickboxing (Sanshou) National Championships.
>
> It wasn't because I was good at punching and kicking. . . . That seemed a bit dangerous, considering I did it on a dare and had four weeks of preparation. Besides, I have a watermelon head—it's a big target.
>
> I won by reading the rules.[1]

Ferriss discovered that most fighters practically ignored the implications of two particular regulations. First, weigh-ins were done the day prior to the event. And second, if a contestant fell off the raised platform three times in a round, he was disqualified. So Ferriss mastered advanced dehydration techniques often used by Olympic wrestlers to lose 28 pounds in 18 hours, allowing him to weigh in at 165 pounds and then rehydrate back to his normal 193 pounds, three full weight classes heavier than his opponents, by fight time. Then it was a matter of physics. Ferriss simply shoved each lighter opponent off the platform three times and won every round including the gold medal match. The judges were not happy, but he had won fair and square.

While Ferriss's opponents might have had more Shanshou skill and practice, he knew the rules and actually *applied* them to competition. We must grasp this same wisdom if we will reap the blessings of God's guidance. Many people know what the Bible says about marriage, child raising, and other family matters. But only those who are willing to apply what they know have a fighting chance at success.

My prayer for you is that you would put into practice anything this book helped you see in Scripture as God's will for your family. Be doers, not just readers (James 1:22). May God be pleased, and may you enjoy the blessings that come from your family working together as a team for God's glory.

Notes

Chapter 1

1. Henry M. Morris, *The Genesis Record* (Grand Rapids, MI: Baker, 2004), 126.

2. See Genesis 4:6–7 for the identical wording where God warns Cain that sin's desire is *for* him (i.e., sin wants to dominate him), but he needs to "rule over it." For further explanation of this interpretation and possible alternatives, see Raymond C. Ortlund Jr.'s "Male-Female Equality and Male Headship: Gen 1–3" in *Recovering Biblical Manhood and Womanhood*, edited by John Piper and Wayne Grudem (Wheaton, IL: Crossway, 1991), 108–09.

3. Morris, *The Genesis Record*, 123.

Chapter 2

1. David Maraniss, *When Pride Still Mattered: A Life of Vince Lombardi* (New York City: Touchstone, 1999), 274.

Chapter 5

1. *Searching for Bobby Fischer*, dir. Steven Zaillian, perf. Max Pomeranc, 1993.

2. Ginger Hubbard, *"Don't Make Me Count to Three!": A Mom's Look at Heart-Oriented Discipline* (Wapwallopen, PA: Shepherd Press, 2004), 26.

Chapter 6

1. Paul David Tripp, *Age of Opportunity* (Phillipsburg, NJ: P&R, 2001), 59.

2. Joshua Harris, *Not Even a Hint* (Sisters, OR: Multnomah, 2003), 23.

3. Stuart Scott and Martha Peace, *The Faithful Parent* (Phillipsburg, NJ: P&R, 2010), 4.

Chapter 7

1. Nancy Wilson, *Why Isn't a Pretty Girl Like You Married? . . . and Other Useful Comments* (Moscow, ID: Canon, 2010), 9–10.

2. Chuck Milian, *We're Just Friends and Other Dating Lies* (Greensboro, NC: New Growth, 2011), 33.

3. Wilson, 95.

4. Milian, 37.

5. "London 2012 Olympics: S Korea's Shin Finds Redemption in Silver," *Taipei Times*, August 6, 2012, http://www.taipeitimes.com/News/sport/archives/2012/08/06/2003539571.

Chapter 8

1. Jay Adams, *Wrinkled but Not Ruined* (Woodruff, SC: Timeless Texts, 1999), 26.

Epilogue

1. Timothy Ferriss, *The Four-Hour Work Week* (New York City: Vermilion, 2011), 28.